A Teen's Guide to the Conversation Game:

How Talking Can Improve Your Popularity, Your Self-Esteem, and Your Life

Kathryn A. T. Knox

Copyright

Foreword

This is a book about talking. It's not about making speeches or doing formal presentations.

Think about the ways words can turn acquaintances into friendships, or how words can make impressions that don't represent who we are. Talking is important. Sure, we all talk, but some converse with others more easily and effectively. How do they do that?

Conversation with others is like a game. In this game, you can practice skills and get better, just like you can with any game.

This book is for you and me and all of us. I hope you enjoy it, and I'd love to hear from you.

The chapters in this book give readers strategies for improving listening and assertive phrasing,

- experiencing better conflict resolution with a 5 step, and 3 step process,
- accepting compliments,
- making real apologies,
- managing small talk and online talk,
- contributing to classroom discussions,
- improving flow and tone of speaking, and
- avoiding conversational traps

Some short dialogues provide practice with these strategies. You may listen at www.RubyMountainPress.com.

Table of Contents

Chapter 1
What's in it for Me?

Talking is conversation.
Conversation is a way for humans to think together.
Conversation helps to build strong relationships.

WHAT'S in it for me (WIIFM)? Good question. Whenever we choose to take on the practice associated with becoming better at a sport or a skill, we have to think WIIFM? Is the time we put into the practice of the skill going to be worth it or have a benefit?

Talking is a skill. Everyone talks and communicates with other people. Some do this skill better than others. You may have some questions about talking. Is it possible to break down and practice skills of communication like you'd do in a sport? Can strong conversation skills make a difference in making and sustaining relationships? Can they help to build our self-esteem and manage our verbal emotions? Can they contribute to getting a good job? The answer to these four questions is YES!

If you've ever watched a show where judges rate performance, you've probably noticed a HUGE difference in contestant's responses to the judges' criticisms. Some of the comments given to the performers are definitely hard to take. But usually, instead of just being defensive or shouting obscenities, or closing up and blaming others, the top finalists step up to the plate and use strong listening and communication to build bridges to the audience and judges, even if they're not chosen as number one. They ask for feedback and they take it so they can improve their ability. How do they do that? How do they use conversation to improve their chances of ongoing success?

Can you think of a person you look forward to seeing, who has interesting things to say, who makes you feel important, and gives you full attention when you're speaking? Though you might feel comfortable talking with one or two people who are your peers, you might feel less comfortable talking with an adult, or being part of a conversation with a group of diverse people you don't know so well. This book helps everyone learn to be a more skilled player in what we can call *The Conversation Game*.

You'll learn to break down conversation into parts that you can think about and practice. In this book, you'll learn specific moves and plays. You'll read and hear simple examples of what "works" and what doesn't, and you'll have the chance to practice easy, guided exercises to help you feel more comfortable talking with other people. This isn't a book about making speeches. It's a book about building relationships and success through conversation.

A game?

You may think right now, "Conversation isn't a game. It's just talking. Some people are good at talking and some aren't." Seems true. However, making conversation has plays and moves anyone can learn and choose to practice. When you know the plays and moves and use them, you become better at being a player in the game. You don't have to be a bystander on the sidelines anymore, wishing you had better conversation skills.

When I was in middle school. . .

When I was in middle school, I was extremely shy. I didn't look forward to meeting new people, or being in a room for a long time with lots of people. I really hated to be called on in class. I often felt at a loss for what to say to someone I didn't know all that well, and even with friends, sometimes there were awkward gaps in conversation.   I didn't want to stand out. On the other hand, I was always having conversations in my head and analyzing them, or thinking about what I should have said. I was worried about how something would sound or how the person I spoke to would perceive me. Have you ever had an experience like that?

I'm sure it was obvious to others that I was uncomfortable or nervous sometimes with my part in the Conversation Game. I didn't know I could try and practice specific things to improve my feelings about talking, and my overall speaking ability. I didn't know all the plays and strategies I could use and of course, I avoided practice.

I remember one time when we had some visitors over to our house. My mom and I sat in the living room with these visitors with hardly ANY conversation going on. Neither my mom nor I had good conversation skills. The time sitting around seemed like forever. It was so AWKWARD! Another time, I went out with someone I didn't know well, and after a few minutes we ran out of things to say. We asked each other a few questions, made a couple of comments about people in the movie we had seen, but overall the communication felt choppy and out of balance. When we did talk, it felt more like an interview than a conversation, with one person asking a question and the other one just answering, followed by a lot of awkward silence.

It is true that when you're not good at something, you don't like to do it. However, like most of us, I had to learn to become better at some things that I didn't like to do. I had to work to be better at playing the Conversation Game with different people and in different situations. It took some years but I did get better—quite a bit better.

A few years ago, I was on a panel in Washington D.C., with several TV cameras around the room filming us. One of the cameras had the CNN label. In the past, I wouldn't have been able to deal with that situation at all. Because I had challenged myself over the years and had worked to use different communication strategies, I found that I felt very comfortable and actually enjoyed that communication opportunity. I wasn't even a bit embarrassed as I reviewed a recorded session that played on television that week, with people from my school.

Since then, I have worked with lots of teams, given presentations to hundreds of people, introduced a mayor and governor, been on radio interviews, done training that lasted many days for hundreds of participants, worked with people overseas, led assemblies, and worked closely with students and their families. I really like speaking and conversation now. What a change!

Because of my improved speaking ability, I have been given many opportunities that have led to a bigger salary at my job and expanded chances to learn and do more. Practicing my conversational skills has helped me SO much. Because these ideas have worked for me, I want to share them with you.

Words are so powerful in building relationship and success. Maya Angelou wrote, "Words mean more than what is set down on paper. It takes the human voice to infuse them with shades of meaning."

And Margaret Wheatley wrote that true conversation is ". . . a timeless and reliable way for humans to think together."

Chapter 2
Getting to Comfort in Conversations

Whether you feel comfortable or awkward talking with others, you can realize that conversation is a game.
People have a role in the game.
Just like in any game, the foundational skills take practice.

CONVERSATION isn't about making speeches or being clever. It's a way for humans to think together, and build relationships by thinking together.

You're reading this because deep inside you want to improve your game. If you've played sports, or performed in music, or worked hard at learning something difficult, you know the value of targeted practice. This improvement will take work and sometimes practice will feel awkward, but you can do the work to become better.

My own conversation skills will always need to improve. I need to work at my practice regularly.

Improving your skills in the game of conversation, will help you in the current responsibilities and roles you have, in school, in your career development, in a job, and in all of your relationships. So much success is based on strong relationships with others, and one huge way to build strong relationships, is through talking.

Even though you may think you don't want to be talking in front of a crowd or TV cameras, you can get to a level of comfort, where no matter WHAT the conversational situation is you can deal with it well. You can learn to play well and feel proud of your ability.   If you don't play well, you might be judged unfairly.   Let me give you a simple example of what I'm talking about.

Ric: "Hey, Ben! I saw your uncle. He said you both took a trip to Colorado to go skiing."
Ben: "Yeah."
Ric: "How was it?"

Ben: "OK."
Ric: "Uh, where did you go?"
Ben: "Breckenridge."
Ric: "Did you have good powder?"
Ben: "Yeah."

It's amazing how much information is shared, and how many impressions happen in a conversation, whether a person says much or not! If you feel uncomfortable with making the plays of the Conversation Game, you can make others feel uncomfortable, awkward or uninteresting, even if you didn't mean to. There were several unspoken messages given to Ric by Ben in this short conversation.

- o Ric might think Ben doesn't want to talk with him (not true).

- o Ric might assume Ben didn't really have that great of a time in Colorado and doesn't want to talk about it (not true).

- o Ric may even think Ben is just sullen or withdrawn (not true).

Those messages wouldn't be based on reality, because Ben actually had an awesome time in Colorado, enjoyed two feet of new champagne powder on top of a four foot base, and tried snowboarding for the first time! So, what happened in that conversation where such potential for misunderstanding was created?

Ben's verbal responses weren't contributing to a good game. He was a weak player responding with single words and giving little information back to Ric to work with. Ben felt awkward talking with a guy who was older than he was and who he didn't know well.

The conversation felt lopsided to both of them. Ric had to hold the interaction together by constantly thinking of questions. That wasn't fun for Ric. Ben might have thought there were too many questions coming his way. That wasn't fun for Ben. The whole game fell apart.

What are some benefits to me?

Being good at playing The Conversation Game is a VERY powerful resource. Conversation connects people with people. When it's done well, good conversation

- o builds bridges between people,

- o makes friendships easier to develop and makes dates more interesting and fun,

- o promotes more equity and respect in relationships,

- o dissolves some misunderstandings,

- o shares and builds accurate information and knowledge,

- o makes employers more impressed with you, and in general, makes others feel less awkward because you're good at the game!

Think of the Game. . .

Have you ever seen a game in which one person throws a ball and then the other person catches it and stands there holding it? Probably not very often.

Most people who play a team game, know the rules of the game they are playing. The rules of a ball game include being able and willing to play to some extent because of personal practice. In a ball game you wouldn't expect to see a player standing alone holding the ball while others on the team wait around for that player to do something. Poor conversations can feel like that, though—like standing and holding a ball while others wait, or even like letting the ball drop in the midst of a game, and then just looking at it lying there. On the other hand, good conversation can feel invigorating like participating in a fun sport!

Let's hear two short conversations. One "works" and the other doesn't. One conversation works because some plays were put into practice, not necessarily because one group is friendlier—though it seems like it to the listener.

First Conversation

Becca: "Hey, Liz!"

Liz: "Hey."
Becca: "Where have you been?"
Liz: "Nowhere." (Looks around at people passing by.)
Becca: "I just came from volleyball practice."
Liz: "Oh." "Huh." (Glances at her phone.)
Becca: "Where are you going now?"
Liz: "Dunno."

Second Conversation

Becca: *"Hey, Simone!"*
Simone: "Hey! Where've you been?"
Becca: "I just got out of volleyball practice."
Simone: "Coach Corn is really tough. Did you make the team?"
Becca: "Yeah, I did." 'I was so amazed that I did."
Simone: "Tell me more about what happened."

The first conversation is out of balance. Because Becca and Liz are friends, it would be a guess that Liz is not trying to make Becca feel awkward, but she just doesn't know what to say because she's gotten into a habit of not playing the game well. She's gotten into the habit of being distracted. Compare the second short conversation to the first one. It's obvious even from these few sentences, that Simone is better at the Conversation Game than is Liz, and that conversation doesn't feel strained.

Chapter 3
Listening and Distractions

We listen with our eyes to other people.
We listen at over 480 words per minute, while we talk at approximately 120 words per minute.
Listening skills are critical to conversation.
We may think we listen all the time, but we can get better at listening.
When we get better at listening, we get better at the Conversation Game.

LISTENING? WHAT DOES listening have to do with making friends, or with conversation? Everything! The well-known speaker and author, Stephen Covey, notes that we *"listen with our eyes."* Because we do listen to others with our eyes, as well as through our own experience and judgments, learning to listen is more challenging than just talking less. In the conversation in the previous chapter, between Liz and Becca, Liz was distracted by people passing by and her phone and just gave one word responses to Becca. Giving one word responses is kind of like throwing the team ball into the air and assuming you're playing the game. Liz wasn't really listening.

People only hear about 25% of what we say. Isn't that surprising? Some people don't take the time to completely hear, while others get distracted. Many other things, such as our body language, our vocal tone, or our eye contact, send clear messages along with the words we speak. Words are just a part of the message we send to other people.

You know what's interesting? People often think you're a good conversationalist if you are a good listener! Some people may think that listening is a passive activity, but it's not. An active listener does all sorts of things including putting questions into his or her mind as someone else is speaking. An active listener pays attention and doesn't interrupt. An active listener monitors his or her thinking to make sure he or she is focusing and not being distracted. An active listener gives respect to the speaker by letting the one speaking, speak, while the listener pays attention.

Do you know that we can listen at over 480 words per minute? When we speak, we talk at only about 120 words a minute. Because we talk less quickly than we can listen, we can easily get distracted or bored. Here are some ways to practice being a good listener and be ready to enter actively into the Game:

Re-focusing

Because so much is going on in our world and in our minds, this exercise can be difficult. Multitasking with technology has contributed to a habit of being half-attentive, too. Refocusing means keeping our thoughts aware and attentive to the present situation. It means not letting our thoughts become distracted, fuzzy, or wander to something else for long. Many of us have a habit of mental wandering when other people talk. We just do. The good news is that we can change that habit. If you were golfing and getting close to the green, you wouldn't look away from the green to see what other people were doing. You'd keep your focus on what was important.

Let's imagine you meet two acquaintances after an event. They are talking about something that happened to one of them. You are kind of interested but half of your mind is moving toward thinking about an assignment you didn't complete, or the clothes someone is wearing, or you keep checking your texts. To refocus, you might have to say something to your consciousness like, "I was texting again! I didn't hear that last bit he said. I need to practice looking up and listening more." Or, you might even discover, "I've been humming that song in my mind, and haven't even heard what the others were talking about!" If you find that when people are talking, you are often thinking of something else, be aware that you will probably need to do some self talk about focusing in the present moment with other people, until it becomes a habit. This can be your first area of practice. If you think this is an area you need to work on, stop now and reflect on how good you are at staying attentive to the talking going on. You could even count how often in an hour of being with someone, you drift out of mental focus. Refocusing is a discipline that requires practice.

Really thinking about "It"

"It" is the whole conversation—the topics, the listening, the body language, the feelings, the connections, the people, the moves, the plays. Suppose you're in a group waiting for a bus. An acquaintance is complaining about a decision about curfew made by the city government. During that complaint, you might catch yourself thinking about something random things like, "I'm hungry. I think I want a salad." and "I like those shoes."

Has that type of thing ever happened to you? I know it has to me. The effort to really listen to someone, rather than rambling along in mental chaos, makes you present in the moment with other people. You may not care about the topic someone is discussing, but you can use the opportunity to listen, to practice refocusing, and to analyze the whole conversation. What is happening with the people playing the game? Who is playing it well and who isn't?

Being curious

This mental exercise can be a challenge if you think you're not interested in too many things. Let's say someone during soccer practice starts talking about something unusual—say, something REALLY unusual like . . .leaf-cutter ants.

leaf cutter ants??

You can either choose to be an active listener and use self talk to keep focus, "She's kind of interesting telling us what she saw in Costa Rica. I'd like to see those ants." Or you can choose to disconnect from listening. You can allow yourself to feel more sophisticated than others and say to yourself with a mental eye roll, "Boooring! What type of person is interested in ants?"

We always have a choice. Your decisions about listening will affect your friendships. When you choose not to play after someone starts a game, that's a powerful but negative message. When you give attention to someone who is talking about something you're not that interested in, you choose to get in the game. You're also giving the message that their thoughts are important and they are important. That's a flattering message: they count enough for you to listen to.

Suppose you enter a conversation where the topic is something you don't know much about--like astronomy, or tennis, or modern sculpture or African politics. Instead of habitually thinking, *"That's boring,"* being disinterested, or letting your thoughts pop around the room to various other things, you could instead choose *"OK, I choose to refocus and be curious about what they are saying."* The response is your choice. G.K. Chesterton wrote, *"There are no uninteresting things, there are only uninterested people."*

Wow. Read that quote again and think about what it means. People are interested in people who engage with them.

Clarity about your values and beliefs

A contestant in a Miss USA competition was asked about how she felt about cosmetic marketing to young kids.   It was obvious that she was trying not to offend anyone, so she wobbled all over the place with her answer.   People would have valued her honesty instead of her prevarication (meaning not really answering the question).   Sure, sometimes you really *don't know* what you think about certain things, and that's OK.   However, many times we really *DO know* what we think about important issues but we don't take a stand and share our thoughts. Why do we hold back?

What is important to you?   What do you strongly believe in?   When you are clear about what is truly important to you, when challenging topics come up, it's easy to be straight with your response because you are clear about your values and beliefs.   You may disagree with something that's been said in a conversation.   It's OK to disagree.   Friends should be able to stand for their own values and beliefs and still remain friends.

People of different ages or backgrounds, cultures or beliefs,   should be able to disagree about a viewpoint or values, and still be respectful and be able to hear one another.   A solid friendship should be able to handle disagreements without falling apart. In fact, for players of the Conversation Game, disagreements can be "spice" and make the plays more interesting.   It's good to have debate and healthy differences. You don't have to be afraid that if you don't agree with everything that is said, that people won't like you.

Even if people don't agree on something, beliefs and values are part of who each person uniquely is. Each person should be able to share what is important to them without feeling intimidated, put down, or pushed out of the Game.

Say someone makes fun of an adult acquaintance who is involved in an environmental action to clean up a city park. If you feel strongly about the issue, you might respond with, "I know you think that Green group isn't going to be able to make any difference with cleaning up the park, but I think it's important to take care of the environment. I like what he's doing. I rock-climb and I wouldn't want a bunch of trash in the mountains." Standing up for your beliefs and values is a good thing. Friends and acquaintances can honor different beliefs without giving up their own. Another friend might respond to your comment, "I can understand where you're coming from, but I don't think people should be wasting time and money on this particular project." Both values are there in the Game. Everyone has the choice to have their voice heard.

Picturing

When you add visual images in your mind while someone is talking, you are adding one more "hook" for your memory. Mental pictures help our focus and our understanding because our brains actually comprehend better and retain information well through visual images. You comprehend better when you include pictures. Have you ever heard the phrase, "A picture is worth a thousand words?" Pictures and visuals help you to summarize and organize information more quickly in your mind, and they help with retrieving information from memory. More examples of how to use picturing to bring ideas to a conversation, will come later in the book!

Connecting

Active listening mentally connects what someone is talking about with something else. The connection could be something you've heard someone else say, a place you've visited, an experience you've had, an emotional event, or something you've heard or read about. For example, if a discussion is going on about a news story of a person adrift in a boat in the Atlantic, you might mentally connect with your family's experience getting lost in a desert during a hike. Connecting can build empathy, and give you something to share if you want to: *"That reminds me of..."*

Making connections in academic areas helps you to remember things that seem abstract, more easily. For example, after listening actively to someone discussing a physics experiment, you might think, *"What she's describing sounds kind of like a roller coaster design."* That type of connection builds your memory and it also makes you think and engage on a whole different level with the speaker.

You can make connections, build pictures, make questions, evaluate your values, refocus and be "full on" the moment – all through active listening. That's why it's so important to the game of conversation.

Think of two ideas to improve your active listening to practice this week. At the end of the week, check your progress and make a new goal.

Oh yes! There is one more topic for this chapter called SELN

Before you enter the playing court of the Conversation Game, always check your physical position, your listening, and your overall attention. Employ **SELN** consciously. This means

- **S**it up slightly if you are sitting, or
- turn toward the person if you are standing;
- make **E**ye contact,
- **L**isten and
- **N**od from time to time.

SELN.

It's easy but it's powerful in conversation. Do it and see what happens. You might be amazed at the results. I once tried this out in a big crowd that was standing, listening to a well-known speaker. I made eye contact and as I listened, I nodded from time to time. That was it. I couldn't believe it, but the speaker started looking at me more and talking directly to me—like I was someone important! A person standing by me also connected in conversation with me as she noticed the speaker's attention moving my way. Both people responded to SELN in action, without any words initially being spoken, and I got the attention of two people. Use SELN during coaching or with a teacher, and see what happens.

How many times I did use SELN today? (Try it a couple of times in class for starters or at a shared family meal during conversation.) What change did I notice in how people listened to me?

Chapter 4
Online Talking

Is online conversation, really conversation?
In online conversation, there are at least 6 poor plays to identify and avoid, then to replace with more effective tools.

SO **MUCH OF** our conversation is online, on varied devices, via social networks, and in school technology. It's a HUGE part of relationship building and learning. We communicate this way all the time but may not really think about how to make online conversation more effective.

In an online video-based discussion group, students listed what some bad communication practices were. Here are some of the items on their list:

○ ignoring the speaker

○ interrupting others and monopolizing

○ not speaking loud enough to hear

o speaking too loudly over other's voices

o fading out of attention and not really listening because of multitasking

o not responding in a timely way

o throwing in some idea that doesn't make sense to the conversation or giving an incomplete response

o using sarcasm, criticism or put downs

EVERYONE in the group agreed that these things were problems in communication and yet many admitted to doing some of those things. They all agreed there was room for personal improvement in the game of online conversation.

Online talking can be complex. It can include all sorts of communication at once, photos, audio and video conversations, texting, adding to discussion threads, and widening the conversation to include other people in the world. Developing a good Game online may include different conversational challenges.

o Have you been in an online conversation where someone obviously wasn't really focusing and you had to repeat information?

o HAVE YOU EVER INTERPRETED A SENTENCE IN ALL CAPS AS BEING ANGRY???

o Have you ever been hurt or felt bullied by something someone wrote?

○ Have you ever texted something quickly and then immediately wanted to take it back, realizing you shouldn't have sent that communication because it might be misinterpreted?

○ Have you been distracted by the quality of your own voice or facial expressions in a video chat?

An acronym is a "word" made of abbreviations or first initials of other words. Acronyms can help us recall ideas or lists. I've changed a list of some poor conversational plays into an acronym so they can be remembered more easily. "**BsmJap**!" B-S-M-J-A-P stands for six poor plays.

Bumping

Bumping is a poor play in the Conversation Game. It essentially means that you wait somewhat passively (generally wandering in thought) until the end of what someone is saying, and then you kind of feel like you just went over a bump because suddenly you are "jerked back to reality" and have to try to "find *something*" to say back. That feeling tends to make you avoid conversation because you so often feel "put on the spot." If you feel "on the spot" a lot, it could be because you're multitasking or holding more than one conversation at a time even if it's in your own head.

Self-absorption

Self-absorption is a state of being totally engaged in thinking of something of interest to you (like the words to a song, or what you're wearing, something you just read on your phone, or your afternoon plans).   Self-absorption is a poor play because it essentially erases one half of the dialogue—the other person's side.

Mmming

This play is just making some sort of noise like "Huh," or "Mmm" or "Mmm mmm," or including some icon or smiley face,   rather than saying something that contributes.   It makes a minimal contribution and if that type of response continues for very long, the other person will get tired of having to hold the whole game up alone.

Jumping

Jumping involves jumping in with something *you* want to say rather than letting the other person have equal time.   This is an aggressive play.   You are taking over before the other person is finished, and maybe even changing the direction of the dialogue to something that focuses on your interests or yourself. For example, Charlie is talking about a movie he saw, and then as soon as there is a break in the talk, you jump in with information about a movie YOU saw and start talking about that.   Jumping can be monopolizing or one-upping someone else.

Advice

Advice can be helpful when asked for, but when someone is talking about something that is bothering him or her, and advice is *not* asked for, it's often a poor play to offer it. For example, if I said, "I'm worried about my brother. He just got this motorcycle and I'm afraid he'll get in an accident." If you jump in with advice, you'd immediately start to tell me what I should do, or what he should do, or what he should not do. Advice isn't really what I wanted *yet* and it can be annoying. You probably don't know enough about the situation. You might want to help, but slow down with quick advice. Listen more first.

Give the conversation a chance to develop before giving unasked for advice. In online conversations especially, you can't read the body language and see the eyes or always hear the tone, so you might need to take a bit more time than you would in face to face conversations, to figure out what is really wanted and when.

Put-down

In using this poor play, the player chooses to make someone feel less important. In choosing to put down someone else, the player may believe he or she will seem more important or interesting. Put downs happen a lot in online conversation. If you have a trusting relationship with someone you can usually figure out if the put down is intentional or not. If you're with a group of people online or talking with someone you don't know very well, it's harder to figure that out. Online or face to face, putdowns can really hurt.

You might be thinking, "These poor plays are not only in online talking, they're in *all talking*." You're right. They especially happen a lot in online talking just because of the distance factor.

Max, Leesha and Mark are chatting and networking with video. Leesha and Mark now Max is interested in all sorts of science. He he was sharing information about his trip to another country. Mark asked a question about Max's trip, and Max responds and also sends along two photos.

Leesha says as she sees the photos come in: **M**mm. (Leesha is feeling bored with Max's story.) She uses "**M**mming" then she shifts the focus of the group from Max to herself using her camera (self-absorption): *"So tell me what I want to hear: People, do you like this shirt?"*

Mark shows interest in his friend's trip and asks some questions about the photos Max sent. He also sends Leesha a quick text to acknowledge her need for attention, *"nice"* Mark is trying to play two games at once.

"Well, Imma science nerd." Max sends an animated robot gif out to his friends.

Leesha: *"Max-Geek, go do something else...you are boring everyone."* Leesha is using the **P**ut-down play. She is giving Max a message that she's not listening and that others shouldn't either. Leesha digs in her backpack for something (and showing the **S** play again says,) *"Oh, here it is. I knew I had some gum in here."* She holds it up to the camera, unwraps it and chews it. "My gum. Too bad you can't have some.

She still resists getting into the Game. The message is that her friends are boring, and the topic is boring, and even a stick of her gum is more worthy of attention.

If you don't want to play the Game with others, if you don't want to listen and you don't want to practice to get better, leave the Game. In any sport, if you choose not to play, you don't keep interrupting play of the ball and then telling everyone, *"Please notice that I'm not playing."*

When you interrupt, distract, show boredom about, or put down topics others have introduced, you are essentially doing the same thing. You're interrupting the throw or catch of the ball and then saying that you didn't really want to play. *"Notice-- I'm not playing!"*

You, because you are reading this right now, are making a commitment to increasing the positive power of conversation in your life. Your decision to improve the power of your conversation will require practice just as any game does, but it's worth it! Every time you catch yourself practicing active listening, using **SELN**, or putting into play any of the other positive moves and plays in the book, give yourself a mental pat on the back and keep on. When you catch yourself using an old bad habit, be glad that you caught yourself and try something better.

Use positive self talk when playing the Game

Know that good listening is a key of success. Tell yourself that when you're really listening, you're not only learning something, you're building a relationship, and you're building a critical communication skill. In short, when it's your turn to talk online, talk. When it's your turn to listen, listen. Don't be thinking of how quickly you can interrupt or change the flow. Don't be thinking about what *you* will say next. Just *listen*. Hear what is being said and be willing to find some interest in what you hear.

Shift attention from yourself to others

If you're always thinking about yourself, or worrying about how others might be thinking of you, it may take some practice to shift your attention, but you can do it.

One issue with audio chats can be difficulty in sustaining a conversation because you can feel like you're talking into empty space. You may get concerned about how your voice is sounding or you find it hard to keep a focus.

People get engaged with visual stimulation. One helpful suggestion to keep a sense of active presence in the conversation (when you're alone!) is to put a mirror in front of your device. Voila, there is a face in the room with you! When you sincerely smile when you're talking, your voice generally takes on a pleasant tone. A mirror reminds you to smile, and it also alerts you to other emotions that might be showing up in your voice. Even though having a mirror around seems like you're focusing on yourself more, over time you'll get used to it, and will have more of a feeling of just another face in the room, and as a subconscious reminder to pay attention to what your facial expressions might be saying to the other person on the line.

Be aware of feelings

You probably know that if you're telling a story and the person you're telling it to looks out the window or interrupts you to talk about something else, you can feel bad. Don't let the same feelings happen to someone else in your conversation with them online.

One word responses to something someone is explaining or sharing, can also feel abrupt or even rude to the other person online. "Wow." "Fun." "Oh." don't invite others to continue a rich conversation. More about one word responses later!

Don't judge the person before he or she has even talked very much.

Give the person a chance, just as you'd like to have a chance to express who you are and share what you believe.

OK, pause here. A lot about listening and poor plays were shared. Go back to review one thing you are choosing to practice improving this week.

Chapter 5
Gambits, Plays and Moves

How do you start a conversation with different people?
How do you keep a conversation going when you don't know much about the person you're talking with?
How can you remember information about people you've met?

A GAMBIT IN chess is an opening play. In chess, a player will often start play with a pawn in order to gain an advantage later. In this book, a gambit is a term we'll use for that bit of conversation that has been offered to start play. You can provide the gambit, or someone else can provide it to you. If you take the offer to play, and play well, you may gain an advantage in how people perceive you both now and later.

Practice and Feedback are the "Breakfast of Champions." Every person who works hard to become good at a sport, at playing a musical instrument, or at speaking, seeks opportunities to analyze practice and gain feedback on how he or she is doing.

Plays and moves

A **play** is how you contribute to or take-away from the Conversation Game by what you *do.*

A **move** is an internal but conscious process when you are questioning, reflecting, planning, or analyzing. It's what you *think.*

A **gambit,** as mentioned above, is a specific opening play.

There are four basic moves that help a person get ready to make a play in response to a conversational gambit:

- ○ Focusing
- ○ Finding clues
- ○ Creating questions
- ○ Following up

Finding clues

This is an important listening move.   When you, as a listener, actively seek clues hiding in the few key things that are given in the gambit, you can either use them to form a question or come back to something later in the Conversation Game. With a clue in hand, you don't have to wait until the speaker ends speaking, and then think "Oh, I have to think of something to say now!"

Here's an example from Joe.　Joe's ga
*can't wait for the weekend!　My cousins
going to go fishing."*

What clues can you pick up from t......
sentences that would lead to more information?　1.
Joe has cousins. 2. Joe likes to fish. 3. He's going
somewhere else to fish.

In this short conversation, you choose to make
the　mental move of focusing and then forming a
question from one of the clues.

- o "Where are you going to fish?"
- o "Do you use flies or bait?"
- o "Do you mostly fish in a river or lake?"
- o "How many cousins do you have?"
- o "Do your cousins live here?"
- o "Have you fished for a long time?

Lots of questions rise to the surface from just a
small number of clues. When questions form in your
mind, it's a *move*.　When you ask someone a
question, it becomes a *play*. You get to choose the
play.　Suddenly, the conversation is starting and
there are questions to keep it going if you choose.

On the other hand, Lacy also heard Joe's gambit,
and thought to herself, *"I don't know anything about
fishing."*　So, when Joe talked, Lacy stood there,
hands in pockets, thinking to herself, "*I don't have
anything to say."* Who is going to have the better
relationship today just from a short conversation?

TMM or TMA

Even if you don't know a lot about a subject or don't have a specific question, this play can really help in the Game.   **TMA** simply means *"tell me about."*   It is good general encouragement to a speaker.   **TMM**   means *"tell me more"* and encourages the speaker to expand on what was said *in whatever way he or she wants to*.   Of course, TMM, because it is a powerful play, should only be used once by itself in a short conversation game because you don't want to slam a person with too many questions as if the conversation were an interview.

TMM or TMA sounds like this: *"Tell me about your team's standing in the league."* Or, *"Tell me more about skateboarding."* Or, *"Tell me about that movie."* Or just an open invitation to *"Tell me about that."*

TMM and TMA says to the speaker, "I want more information and you are encouraged to tell me whatever you want to, whatever details you would like to add, or what you think I need to know to continue the game. Here is another example of a gambit, move, and play with TMA:

Gambit:

"I just got back from Ethiopia."

Listeners' moves:

42

I'm focusing. I'm listening. Why did he
Ethiopia is in northern Africa, I think,-nc
What did he do there? I'll use SELN anc

Listener's Play:

"Wow, that must have been a really interesting trip! I don't know much about that part of Africa. Tell me about your trip and what you did."

Much better response than just saying, "Oh, cool." The conversation, with moves based on the **gambit** with the **TMA** play, is on its way. The speaker will give more more clues to play off of in response, and the conversation can continue on smoothly.

If someone uses the **TMM** or **TMA** play *with you*, don't worry about where to start. "Tell me about your vacation." You could highlight a few things that happened in chronological order. ("First we did this, then we did that, and then something else happened"). OR, you might want to picture a few balloons with a different part of the experience or story, in each balloon ("We had a great time at X and this is what happened in each part of the experience.")

Nod

The nod is very powerful non-verbal communication as we mentioned with the SELN play. Nods can keep people talking. The nod says all sorts of things to the receiver, including,

- ○ *"I'm with you."*
- ○ *"I understand."*

- ○ *"Keep going."* and
- ○ *"I hear you."*

Those are all powerful messages to receive and to give.

What, When, Where or How?

What, Where, When or *How* are plays that seek out specific information about time, location, event and action. They can be combined easily with other plays like TMM. These types of questions sound like, "What was the name of that group you said you liked?" "When did you go to Quebec?" "Where is your favorite skateboarding ramp? Why is it so good?" "How do you keep all the Greek characters in the play straight? " "How did you get interested in Manga?"

I have worked with many people who defend or justify the negative habits they've gotten into. They defend lack of skill with diverse conversation. *"I'm just shy."* *"I don't like to talk."* *"I'm not good at small talk."* They have weak plays and don't work at improving their skill. For instance, a person might respond to something they mumbled unclearly, (and which another person asked for clarification about), with just *"Never mind,"* (thus dropping the ball— *thud!*). Or, a person might continue to use vague vocabulary over and over *("yeah." "hmm." "great.")*. Or, a person might use inappropriate language with different listeners just because *"That's how I talk!"* Or, a person might be in the habit of being distracted or interrupting others the majority of time in conversation. "I can't help it!"

Some individuals continue to resist improving the critical skill of being able to talk forthrightly and with attention to diverse people on different topics. No player gets better by ignoring constructive criticism. Be honest with yourself. If your conversational skills aren't where you want them to be, work on improvement in at least one area.

Shy or Introverted?

You may think you're shy. Maybe you're not. Maybe you're just in the habit of thinking you're shy, when you have a preference for more quiet, less-stimulating environments. Being shy means being afraid that someone will judge you. Being shy is being anxious. Being shy is being submissive.

Ted Rubin said that with relationships, like muscles, the more you engage them, the stronger they become. Consider whether you are really shy and anxious, or are just more thoughtful and reflective. You don't have to be someone you're not, but being shy is very different from having a preference for introversion and reflection. Shyness is a liability. Introversion can be a contribution.

- o Do you avoid talking to people due to fear of judgment, or do you just prefer conversations that are one-on-one or in smaller groups?
- o Do you avoid sharing your thoughts with others, or do you feel comfortable expressing

ideas in your conversations especially after you've had time to think about what's being said?

○ Do you feel anxious when you're alone, or do you enjoy solitude when it happens?

○ Do you secretly desire to work on problems with a group of people, or are you comfortable working and figuring out problems by yourself?

If you choose the first part of each sentence above, you may be shy. If you choose the second part of each sentence above you're probably showing a preference for introversion.

There's nothing wrong with being a more quiet or reflective person. Susan Cain has a book you'll

enjoy   that will provoke good extendₑ
about this idea. The book is called *Quiet:*
of Introverts in a World That Can't Stop
Sometimes the best conversations are tho
come from thoughtful engagement and   ⌐
listening.   Cain also argues that different cultures
can misunderstand and undervalue thc capabilities of
introverted people.

If you identify yourself as habitually shy, use
some of the ideas in this book to expand your skills.
Do it for yourself because you want to strengthen
the muscles of your life skills.   If you are thinking
you are really more introverted than shy, learn about
other successful people who were introverted and
introverted traits that are strengths.   Read Cain's
book. There is nothing wrong with a preference for
being introverted, and in fact, introverts bring a lot
to the conversational table.   Their voices and ideas
come from reflection and are often powerful, so
appreciate what you have and continue to strengthen
the muscles of your life preference.

Here are a few other things to think about to
really "polish" your game.

Vocal tone

Vocal tone is important in conversation just as it
is in singing. What do you need to do to make your
voice nice to listen to? Record your voice talking
about something you like to do, and analyze what
you're hearing. Should you

47

- ○ Lower the pitch of your voice just a bit?
- ○ Lower the volume of your voice if it seems too loud or if others have told you that you speak too loudly?
- ○ Raise your voice if people say you speak too softly or if your voice seems muffled?

Later in this book there are practice exercises to improve vocal tone, rhythm, speed, and so on.

Vocabulary and conversation

Do you know that most of us use fewer than 1000 words in our daily conversations? Many dictionaries have 40,000 to 60,000 word entries, and the Oxford English Dictionary has over 171,000 words! There are a lot of words out there we're not even thinking about. We're missing a lot of creative expression by limiting our vocabulary.

A way to start to infuse your language with more interest is to use sensory adjectives. Sensory adjectives and strong verbs make the listener almost smell, see, touch, hear what happened: *"Those cookies you made sizzled like hot caramel corn. Soo great!"* Ok, so that might be *a bit* beyond your comfort zone, but you get the idea. Description is more interesting to listen to than, *"The cookies were good."*

Also add more precise vocabulary into your conversation if you rely too much on repeating flat words like "cool" and "hot" and "great" and "stuff" and "fine" and "weird" and "awesome" and "boring"?

If you discover that you enjoy playing with language, you might even start a new trend with your friends by using multisyllabic words like these below (some of which are found on high-stakes exams):

- "Jane is so *truculent!*" (defiant, aggressive and ready to fight)
- "This is a *bucolic* camp!" (The camp is pastoral and rustic.)
- "He's really showing a lot of *hubris* these days." (arrogant conceit)
- "That piece of art you created was *daedalian*!" (seems hard to do)
- "Aren't you *euphoric* about the concert?" (very happy)
- "I'm totally *fisselig!*" (this word's origin is out of use but it's interesting! It's German and means flustered to the point of incompetence)

Or, if you are *very brave* or have tolerant friends, you might even really extend this idea of interesting vocabulary to employ some old and forgotten English terms into your group speak like, "My cousin is somewhat of a *dorbel*." (someone pretending to be very scholastic). Using more precise or even obtuse vocabulary can be fun (and humorous). Or even engage in phrases from other countries like these examples:

- *boketto* (Japanese) meaning the act of gazing vacantly into space

- *echarse flores* (Spanish), "throwing flowers to oneself" or in other words telling people how good you are
- *tubli* (Estonian)—a person who is hard-working, organized, strong, and has integrity

Listen to your coaches and speak up!

Everyone who gives you feedback is a coach. In a basketball game for instance, you wouldn't say, *"That's just how I am, the others on the team will just have to deal with it."* Or, if you are part of a marching band, you wouldn't reply to some criticism of play that is too soft, *"Well, I don't feel like playing louder."* You'd listen to your coach and work to improve or you probably wouldn't be on the team or in the band much longer.

Remember, if you are a soft speaker, your ears are closer to your mouth than other people's ears are! If you are used to mumbling or muttering, care enough about your listeners to work on improving your clarity so that others don't have to work so hard to hear. On the other hand, if you talk too loudly or are bombastic (go ahead and look the word up), tone it down.

Use "contact cards"

One technique that can be very helpful as you build your background knowledge about other people so you can reference information or ask questions when you see them again, is called a contact card. Use your address book or contacts list on your device, and simply add notes to names of friends and acquaintances. (Of course you can use paper notes or index cards, or whatever you want to use.) Here are some sample notes. You can add to them as you learn more over time.

- o Ted's brother working internship in Morocco. Likes to fish; caught a 3 lb trout. Got lost in the desert; was on TV competition. Visited tallest building in world, likes algebra; 4 sisters
- o Mandy --Loves coral, both color and reefs; birthday November 20; vacation to DC in June, fav. author Austen; two older brothers. Wants a motorcycle. Wants to be oceanographer in Great Barrier reef area in future.
- o Rand collects unusual rocks, plays Lacrosse really well; sister in hospital for a week March 5. Wants to go to France and learn French; draws exotic cars.
- o Tawni --going on a trip to South Dakota where step-brother lives, loves yellow roses. Wants to be environmental architect. Plays in a band. Great cook of Thai food.

You see how you begin to gather and then to use notes? You keep adding to the notes section as you learn more about your friends and acquaintances. They become a good reference for conversations with people you haven't seen in awhile, too.

Think about how you can use this information effectively.

o If Mandy loves the color coral and her birthday is coming up you can get her something in that color.   Or, if you read about coral bleaching in the Great Barrier reef, you can send the article to her, or use it as a starter for a future conversation.

o If you hear some current news about Morocco, you can tie it in with a conversation with Ted.

o When you see Rand, you can be sure to ask about his sister and how she's doing, or share some news about France that you heard about.

As you use this tool, you may find that it helps your memory, because there are so many things to remember over periods of time, especially if you haven't seen someone for awhile. You have a tool to help you keep some important details about friends and acquaintances at hand, to enrich present conversations or references for future ones.   When you remember details about another person's life , that person feels very special and it adds another positive level to the relationship and conversation.

Adding who you are to The Game and developing PMA

Your character influences everything you do, every decision you make, and every conversation you have. A good speaker starts from a position of *positive mental attitude* or PMA.

Positive mental attitude comes from qualities that every person can put into practice. Positive mental attitude will increase your own success in every aspect of life and make your life and your conversations much more interesting. Positive mental attitude is powerful!

A man named Napoleon Hill did research to discover keys of personal success at the turn of the century. (Other more recent books like *The 7 Habits of Highly Effective Teens* by S. Covey, have expanded on this idea.) Eleven of the personal qualities he discovered that lead to success in conversations include:

1. *Tolerance for other's opinions, or slower speech*
2. *Alertness to what others are saying as well as what they are not saying (focusing)*
3. *Courtesy, being kind and patient, allowing others to have the floor as well as you (not interrupting, jumping, or monopolizing)*
4. *Caring about other people (being interested)*
5. *A pleasant tone of voice*
6. *Sincerity (wanting to play the Game)*
7. *Humility of the heart*
8. *A sense of humor*
9. *Smiling*
10. *Enthusiasm*
11. *Control of emotions and temper*

Take a moment to reflect on a couple of these qualities of a positive mental attitude, and think why they're important in playing the Conversation Game. Why would tolerance for other's opinions or slower speech be important in a good conversation? (How would you like to be treated if the person having trouble getting their thoughts together was you?) How about a sense of humor? What does a good sense of humor look like in conversation when it works? How does it add to the relationship? Why is a smile important? What does a sincere smile convey to others? How do you express caring during talking?

Why would control of your temper make a big difference in conversation?

Read the positive mental attitude list again. With each item in the list, ask yourself how *you* express that attitude regularly. If you're not sure, ask your parents or someone you trust for feedback. If you aren't good at the attitude or skill, work on it and then ask for more feedback.

Just as a star tennis player visualizes making the perfect return of a volley, visualize yourself talking with someone you find hard to talk to, with a positive attitude and using effective moves and plays. Imagine yourself becoming better and better at the skill of conversation.

Stop for five minutes, and choose one idea for improvement in conversations in the next two weeks.

- o What I'm going to work on is:
- o How I'm going to know if I've improved:

The Johari window

On some notes I took in a psychology class, I have a drawing of a window with four quadrants. The window diagram is called the Johari window. (It was named for two people who developed the model: **Jo**seph Luft and **Har**ry **I**ngham.)

One quadrant is called *"the open self."* This is the part of us that we share with others and how much of ourselves we let others know about.

Another quadrant is *"the blind self."* This is something others see but something we don't.

The third quadrant is called *"the hidden self."* This self is all that we hide from others.

The fourth quadrant is titled *"the unknown self."* It's what we don't know about ourselves.

A helpful exercise in self-improvement in conversation, is to think about how big each part of that window is. Is your blind self or your unknown self bigger than your open self? What can you do to make your open self wider and deeper with more people?   To open part of your unknown self and become more aware, ask someone you trust for feedback about your character and impression in conversation.

Suggested exercise: Make your own Johari Window and ask for feedback from a coach you trust. Do they have the same impressions about you that you do? Do they see something in the unknown self quadrant that we don't? Regular practice along with feedback are the breakfast of **champions** in any game!

Chapter 6
Gimme Two

Taking turns can seem awkward.
Balance in a conversational game that includes talk, attention,
finding clues, listening and changing topics, develops smoothly with
the right practice.

IN THE SHORT EXAMPLE below, Shara is thinking Marti doesn't want to talk to her (not true).

:sn't want to ask another question because
ımes Marti's annoyed (not true;)

How was science class?"
dunno. . . something about the periodic ...whatever."

There are more plays in addition to the ones already mentioned, that contribute to your ability to play the Conversation Game well, and that are easy to try. One of these is called **Gimme Two**. Gimme Two is easy to practice! It simply means that you make an agreement with yourself that you'll give out *at least two* comments or bits of information in your response. For Marti in the previous example, she might have said, "We learned about the periodic, whatever..., and how selenium is pretty toxic." Shara would then have had at least one clue to play to move the conversation forward with a play like, "What is selenium?"

Here are two more examples of conversation. The two girls in the short conversation below are friends, but live in different areas of the state, and don't see each other as regularly as they'd like to.

Lacy: "How was your trip?"
Marcee: "It was OK."
Lacy: "Weren't you in South Dakota?"
Marcee: "Yeah."
Lacy: "Oh."

Kind of boring yes? Feels kind of awkward for Lacy? Let's break down what's happening:

- Lacy: *"How was your trip?"*
- Marcee: *"It was OK."* (Marcee is making Lacy ask for more rather than simply giving her something, some clue, to work with. She only responds with one short phrase.)
- Lacy: *"Weren't you in South Dakota?"* (Lacy knows that she was, but there is no clue for her to use to ask much else.)
- Marcee: *"Yeah."* (Marcee smiles, but things are getting dull already! She had a good time, but you'd never know it.)
- Lacy: *"Oh."* (She's searching for a way to keep the conversation going. Marcee only gave her

one word. Lacy has to work to get any information at all. Lacy is her friend, but she doesn't like having to do all the digging to keep the Game going. She starts to feel like an interrogator and thus she stops asking.)

What went wrong? How do you think Lacy is feeling? She's probably feeling that the conversation is like pulling teeth one by one, and it will be too painful to go much farther. On the other hand, Marcee may be wanting Lacy to keep asking her questions, but is that really fair? Marcee is a passive player in this game. It's not much fun to play.

Here's another short conversation with the same two girls, but with the "Gimme Four" play added by Marcee. This time Lacy and Marcee are discussing a place Marcee went to on her vacation called Ice-Man Ice. Let's listen.

Lacy: "What is Ice-Man Ice?"
Marcee: "It is this little place that looks like a small garage. It's painted lots of colors like a rainbow, and inside they have

all kinds of shaved ice.I tried five kinds but either blueberry or macadamia nut with coconut ice cream was my favorite."

Marcee is a better player now. She gives Lacy more than a word or phrase in response to her question. There are lots of ways Lacy can choose to put some plays into the Game from the clues given. The conversation became so much easier for Lacy to engage in!

Sure, it can be a little bit risky to share personal information because someone may choose "not to pick up" any of the shared information, or act bored and discontinue the game, and that feels bad. But, if that happens, don't give up. Move on with someone else and try again. Maybe someone is just having a bad day. Gimme Two is a good play to get things started and to keep things going throughout the conversation.

Sanborn: "Hey, what 'cha reading?"

Byron: "I was just checking the hockey standings. NHL training camps start soon. I play virtual hockey so I like to keep up on any information that might influence the outcome."

Sanborn can now make many plays based on the clues given:

> Tell me about the team you like.
> or "Do you play virtual hockey too?"
> or "Tell me about what you're finding in the standings."
> or "Who is your favorite player? Tell me why."
> or "Where are the training camps this year?"

Of course Sanborn wouldn't ask ALL these questions! This is just a list of play options that are available from one rich gambit given by Byron.

Here is another example of you using the Gimme Two play in a different situation:

Your Mom: *"I wanted you to meet Mrs. Crawford. She's a librarian."*

You: *"Hi Mrs. Crawford. So you're a librarian? . . .*(You repeat the person's name to help you remember it and what you heard, which shows you were listening. You use Gimme Two so the person you are introduced to has something to work with.)

- o *I love books.*
- o *I just read David Copperfield.*

Mrs. Crawford now has two clues that you gave her and she can choose to pick up on. Also, because you have the clue that she's a librarian, you could also use a play like one of the following to advance the conversation with her:

- *"What kinds of books are checked out most often?"*
- *"I like Dickens' descriptions of people. Do you have a favorite Dickens' character"*   or
- *"What do you like most about your job?"*

You are both ready to play and can play on as long as you choose. That was easy!

When you are ready to give something to the other person to work with, and also to ask a question, you are opening yourself to the Game. You can learn to talk with ANYONE. That would be an amazing skill to have!! You are showing you can play the Game with all sorts of different players even if you don't know much about them. You are also giving a good impression of yourself as someone who can play the Game well.

If you want to get beyond using basic plays, you can prepare ahead of time to think about different interests or jobs and come up with two or three questions about those. For instance, imagine that you are introduced to someone with the following background or skills: "This is X., a ..... (choose one occupation)"

- LaCrosse player
- Atmospheric scientist or someone who likes watching the stars through a telescope
- Trumpeter in a band
- New mom
- Musician
- A rock collector

- Elementary teacher or someone who wants to be a teacher
- Exchange student from Kazakhstan
- Rodeo competitor

You have a choice. You can say "Hi" and stand there and wait for them to start the play and wonder what you could *possibly* say to them, feeling awkward, OR . . .you could know that you've already practiced and **you are ready**. Think of two questions you might ask of each person listed above. You know some basic plays including focusing, Gimme Two, using clues, the How and What play, and TMA. Now, imagine putting a play into action.

Changing topics—how does that happen?

After having the play focus on one player for awhile, it's then time for a turn to a topic focused on the other player. **Turn-taking** is a crucial play in the Conversation Game. Turn-taking is the back and forth play of the ball in the game. One person may get the basketball and dribble down the court for awhile, but soon it is that player's turn to pass to a teammate. Turn-taking is just like this. If one player keeps the focus on his or her topic and then does not do the turn-taking play, the other person feels left out. Or, if someone gets tired of talking about one topic and just starts talking about something else, especially related to self, that's a poor play that jumps over the topic too quickly. If you start to monopolize, others will zone out or feel irritated. The Conversation Game rules include smoothly "passing the ball" of words and topics.

Marco has been practicing plays in the Conversation Game. He's working on the Gimme Two play and on turn-taking. Marco and Lily are really off to a great start. Turn-taking is really just respect for others' experiences and ideas. It's fun to keep talking about yourself, but when you let others have a turn, you let them have some power. You act fairly. You put equality into action. You give opportunity for mutual appreciation of knowledge. What do you notice is working in the conversation below? When does Turn Taking happen? Do you think there is good listening evident?

Marco: "What are you reading?"
Lily: "The training schedule. Season is about to start so I'm gonna be training hard."
Marco: "What's one of the hardest things about the training season?"
Lily: "Balancing school work and sports."

Marco: "Yeah. It must be hard to have to practice after school for hours and then still have to do homework."
Lily: "Too right! And Coach is expanding my leadership role on varsity this year."
Marco: "How do you feel about that change?"
   or "Tell me more about your leadership role."
   or "Do you want to play next year?
   or "Do you have plans to continue to play after high school?"

Marco used to think he was shy, but he sure doesn't seem shy now in his conversation. A person who thinks of himself or herself as "shy" may really be using that term as a cover for having insufficient practice with the rules of the Conversation Game, especially Gimme Two and Turn-Taking. In the examples, it didn't take much for Marcee or Marco to move away from the limitations of conversational shyness and into easier talking with acquaintances or friends. They just needed some practice with moves and plays.

Zeze: "What did you buy Ruvini for her birthday?"

66

Sheri: "A necklace. I made it. The necklace has this little silver heart that says 'peace' on it. I thought she'd like that because she does yoga."
Zeze: "Oh, you always think of something personal and special. How did you make that heart?"

You saw how Sheri expanded Gimme Two to Gimme *Three*? Zeze has clues to pick up on to keep the conversation going. She is skilled. She gives Sheri a compliment and makes a play from a clue she was given. When you put plays into practice, the conversation is off to a smooth and painless start.

No one likes to play an instrument in front of others if the notes haven't been learned because the player hasn't practiced. No one wants to go on the basketball court if they haven't practiced. So, the answer is. . .*practice*! Start with one play like *Gimme Two, SELN, TMM,* and then add more plays. You can become interested, and interesting, in conversation.

Review the previous discussion about being shy or introverted in the book. Commit to building your conversational muscles from a point of strength instead of anxiety.

Stop and reflect
When I nod and make eye contact, I notice that others _____.

When I use **TMA** or **Gimme Two** instead of waiting for the other person to keep the Game going, I realize _____.

I'm noticing an increase in attention or people interested in talking with me when _____.

When I prepare for a conversation situation, I notice _____.

One idea I'm using is _____.

Chapter 7
What About Those Difficult Conversations?

What do you do when you encounter people who blame, justify, disagree, get defensive?
How do you promote win-win in the Game?

EVERYONE HAS TIMES when a conversation gets difficult or adversarial. What do you do with that? You can choose to

- ○ disengage from talking and be passive, OR
- ○ get adversarial, OR
- ○ act superior as if the other person isn't worth talking to, OR
- ○ choose to play "win-win"

What is win-win? Stephen Covey and others have written about keeping a win-win attitude. This means that both parties feel a personal positive "win," and there is not one person winning and another losing. To keep a win-win attitude, try to understand what the person is saying and/or where   he or she is "coming from." Seek to understand what might have contributed to this person's attitude or belief, without either giving in or fighting.

Separate intent

Conflict will happen. When it does, *don't assume the other person's intent.* Maybe what you're feeling or thinking in a conversation, isn't really the intent the speaker wanted to convey. Maybe the person didn't think what he or she said would have an emotional impact on you directly. Separate your feelings from what you think the person's intent is.

Playing win-win means that you desire to maintain the other person's respect and dignity. One way to think about how to talk to others who are seeming to be difficult, is to spend some time in reflection. Be honest with yourself and seek any potential contributions you might have made to the current difficult conversation:

- o Are you overbearing sometimes with this person?
- o Are you generally more concerned about being liked than about telling what you really think?
- o Do you often worry what others might say about you?
- o Do you have difficulty showing appreciation for other's points of view?
- o Do you sometimes ignore comments that you find offensive?

- ○ Do you find yourself getting kind of aggressive or snippy if people don't agree with you?

If the answers to some of these questions are "yes" perhaps you are not experiencing win-win conversations in which both participant's ideas and values are respected while maintaining friendship and mutual dignity.

One way to work toward win-win discussions is to use some tools like **door-openers**. Here are some examples.

- ○ *"I think I understand what you're saying/where you're coming from. . ."* (This sentence affirms that you've heard the other person; then, you can disagree or share your ideas too.)
- ○ *"Can you tell me more about what you're thinking?"* (You're valuing the other person by asking for more information rather than jumping to conclusions.)
- ○ *"Why do you think that way? I'd like to understand."* or *"Why did you think you needed to tell me all this?"* (You're seeking first to understand before you ask others to understand you.)
- ○ *"I can see your point. I don't agree with you about that."* (You acknowledge the other's point of view calmly, saying you heard and understand but have a different way of seeing things.)

That "but" word

ou ever had a conversation where you say something positive, but to your the response turned back on you in a ay? How did that happen? Look at these examples.

"You explained it well, **but**...I didn't remember what you said." *The person will hear the second part of the sentence—that you didn't remember what they said.*

"I was going to finish the work on time, **but**...I was busy and didn't have time." *The person will just hear the excuse.*

"You did a great job on stage, **but**... part of the solo was off key." *The person will mostly hear how you thought their solo was off key.*

What do all three examples above have in common? Right—the word "but." The but word in a sentence can negate a positive comment that came before. Look at the first part of each example, before the comma. Each compliment is clearly a compliment:

"You explained it well."

"You did a great job on stage."

Then, as soon as the word **"but"** comes into the sentence, something happens. The word "but" is a turnaround word. It deletes the positive that came before because it sounds to the listener like "not really." *That little word cancels the positive or harmless comment you started with.* People seem to hear the words that come after the but first.

So what can you do? Change the word "but" to the word "and." It's amazing what one little word can do to flip the feeling of the conversation.

"You did a great job on stage during practice. Before the performance, work on the one off key bit in the final solo." *The person will first hear they did a great job on stage AND recognize there is an area to improve on. Not a big deal.*

BUT is a de-connector that deletes the good statement that went before.

AND is a connector that helps move the conversation forward with constructive solutions.

Five negative moves

Having a difficult conversation won't be easy. With the right tools, we can at least try to control the process and make it a reasonable one. There are five negative mental moves that can occur when we engage with a difficult conversation. These are

1. to get defensive,
2. to blame the other person,
3. to justify ourselves,
4. to deny our part in the emotional fallout of the conversation, or
5. to leave or give up on further conversation.

Getting Defensive

We may *feel* emotional or angry but that doesn't mean the person was *trying to make us feel* emotional or angry. When we define their purpose as trying to manipulate our emotions, we immediately become defensive. Maybe the intention of the person was just to share information or their perspective, and we took it in an emotional way. When you can separate the intention from the communication's effect on you, you're on your way to controlling the plays and the process of the Game.

Blaming others

Another negative mental move is to blame the other person for your feelings and reactions, and use messages like *"He/she is always thinking he or she* knows the answer!"   "*You (he/she) make me so mad!"* "*You told me that because you knew I'd be upset!"*   or   "*She is the one with the problem!"* Blame may sound aggressive, but it actually says "I am a victim because I can't do anything about how they control my emotions and the situation."

Justifying

A third negative mental move is to justify ourselves and immediately think, "I'm right and you're wrong." When we think this way, we shut off the moves that could help us improve the Game in which we're involved.   If we justify ourselves, we don't examine our feelings and behaviors. We don't consider that we might have been wrong in some way.   We don't give the other person listening time. We indulge our feelings, *"I'm furious with her insensitivity!" "He doesn't get it!"* "I'm totally right! *Everyone thinks that way except you!"*   This approach just keeps the emotions high on the field.

Denying

A fourth negative move is denial. "I had nothing to do with that." "Don't blame me for how you feel." You are disconnecting from something you did that has affected someone else. Denying is a type of passive negative move. "Not me."

Giving Up or Leaving

A fifth negative move is just to disconnect mentally or physically for a difficult conversation. "I can't hear you." "Don't want to play."

Flip the feelings

When you experience these types of mental moves, recognize that they exist but try not to indulge them too much. Realize your response may not be accurate.   Emotions interfere with communication.   Flip the feelings and then, use assertive communication.   Phrases like the ones below can help us stay out of negative moves and emotional reactions so conversation can move forward.

- o *"This is hard for me to hear."*
- o *"I don't know how I feel about this right now."*
- o *"I'm feeling pretty angry as I'm sure you must know."*
- o *"I need a little time to calm down. I'll be back in a few minutes." (You clarify why you are leaving, but also note you're not disconnecting for long.)*
- o *"I am so on the opposite side of this issue, I don't know where to go with it."*
- o *"It seems you're saying (X) which felt like an insult."*
- o *"Let's go back to review the facts instead of arguing from all these opinions."*

Here are a few other things you can try in a difficult conversation:

- o You can shift from judging and reacting, to looking at the situation with curiosity or even compassion, as if you were observing the conversation from a distance.
- o You can say you need some time to think about things. (You don't need to respond immediately when feelings are complex.)
- o You can say what is true for you.
- o You and work to separate intent from impact on you, and be aware that sometimes we take things personally that we shouldn't let become personal. Be a duck. Water can cover the duck completely but it doesn't soak or sink the duck.
- o You can focus on the conversation and actions assertively, rather than attacking the person. You can choose to participate in civil discourse rather than in aggressive win-lose discourse.

Overall, and in truth, the only person you can really change is yourself. You are never in a situation that is so difficult that you can't change your thinking. When you change your thinking, you also change your response. When you change your negative moves and plays, you are no longer a victim or a passive receiver of whatever comes your way.

The Idiot Slap

"You're an idiot!"

"No, *you* are the idiot!"

"He is..."   "She is..." "They are..."

You've probably noticed there is a trend to move from a comment about an issue, to "slap" a person who is making a comment or blogging about an issue. This type of slap-reaction shifts the focus from the issue to personality and then the conversation becomes mushy and unfocused and it loses power. Personal attack in person or online is like someone slapping at you as a bully. The reaction stops conversation.   You mentally turn your back or hit back.   Ignorance and emotion continues. Ideas and issues fall to the ground.

His ideas and comments are just as important as your ideas for consideration and analysis. Your ideas are just as important as hers and are opportunities to refine and review your own understanding.   We may not agree, but slapping around loses the focus.

Threats, big shows, anger, meanness, insulting, blaming, ongoing resentments and comments of revenge don't progress any conversation or thinking. Choosing to engage in sustained discourse in contrast, is an act of courage. Why? Because you are willing to put your own ideas on the table for review and analysis. You can be willing to consider another's ideas with goodwill and without immediate personal judgment. You don't have to agree. Civil discourse allows conversation to continue and go deeper. It's fun and challenging to develop rich discourse. It's part of sustaining a democratic system. Such skill brings liberty from simple, cowardly verbal assault.

Try addressing some of these questions in commentary and conversation.

- o What is the real issue (not a person) to deal with?
- o What is your solution? Why is it the better solution?
- o What is the history of the situation that impacts the present?
- o Where are the logical flaws you see in the discussion?
- o What's your personal story that informs your current understanding?
- o What information do you have to share that is important?
- o How do we move forward effectively from here?

You are always at choice.

Viktor Frankl was in a concentration camp in World War II. Most of his family were killed. He and others were treated terribly. One day, the story was that his face was pushed down into the cold mud under the boot of a Nazi guard. After that experience, he realized that he could always choose how he thought and reacted. That idea the he was always free to choose his thoughts and emotions, gave him freedom the Nazi soldier didn't have--even in the concentration camp. He could choose to hate or not. If Viktor Frankl could do that in a concentration camp, we can certainly do better in our lives. (By the way, if you're interested in reading his outstanding book, it's called *Man's Search for Meaning*.)

Chapter 8
5 Step, 3 Step Conflict Solving

Have you ever been in a conversational situation that turned emotional right from the start?
It doesn't take much to receive a simple statement as a flash of irritation. When that happens, relationships are affected.
In this chapter, you'll learn two extremely important conversational skills.
One is the five-part conflict manager. The other is the three-part apology. You'll also get some ideas on solving conflicts with parents. All of these skills helps anyone to diffuse conflict early without either losing it aggressively, or swallowing feelings.

HAVE YOU EVER been in a situation where what came out of the conversation was totally different from what you thought it should it should have been? Have you ever felt you needed to give or receive an apology but *"Sorry,"* wasn't enough?

Five step conflict management

We might get annoyed, angry, or defensive in communication because we know there's something more that should be said or done. We may want to yell, call someone a name, become aggressive, or even just stop communicating with that person. Or, because we don't know what to do, we may end up acting as if nothing was wrong even though inside we're seething with emotion.

Here are examples of how things can fall apart quickly

You say Hi, to a friend named Marcus. He walks by without saying anything. The next day, Marcus says hi to you. You get a bit confrontational.

"Oh, NOW you say hi!"

What is happening here? Assumptions colored the two greetings. Just two simple greeting opportunities, but because something wasn't clear in the greeting, assumptions were made that caused hurt. You thought he was ignoring you. He now thinks you're mad. At this moment, there is a big opportunity for either escalation or solution.

Let's use a simple step process to help the communication move from confrontation to solution.

Step one: saw!

Tell the person what you observed yesterday. Just the facts--what was seen. In this case, it could be something like,

"Yesterday, I said 'hi' to you and you walked past me."

82

Step two: what?

You ask what happened. You can choose to share what you thought might have been the problem but without confrontation in your voice.

"So, what happened? Did you not see me or did you have something on your mind?"

Step three: wondered

(optional if you get a good answer to step 2.) You dig deeper if step two isn't adequate or if it feels evasive. For instance, with Marcus, you could say

"I wondered if you were mad at something."

"I wondered if you were mad at someone."

"I wondered if the coach got on your case."

"I wondered if you were distracted for some reason."

Step four: uncover emotion and thought

(This step is optional--use it depending on the response you get above.)

Sometimes you can erase the problem in just two steps and some open conversation. Other times, it seems like there is still evasion and you need to dig more deeply without being aggressive. You can share what YOU were thinking or feeling.

"I thought you were avoiding me."

"I felt confused yesterday."

Step five: check in

Checking in is just a closure; a double check that you both can move forward with more clarity and without anger, frustration or annoyance.

"Just wanted to check in with you; make sure we're ok."

Let's try working through the steps again with another scenario. You have tickets to a concert. You invited a friend. You agreed to meet 30 minutes before the doors opened. It's now 5 minutes before the doors open. Your friend rushes up, smiles, and says, *"Sorry I'm late!"* You are really , really, annoyed when you had hoped to be excited. You want to lash out at your friend's perceived insensitivity, but instead you try the five step flow.

○ Step one: **saw**! (the facts)

"We said we'd meet 30 minutes ahead of the show. Now it's 5 minutes till the start."
"I looked at the time, so I didn't know what to think."
"You didn't text me about being late."
Your friend will need to respond to the facts of what you saw and experienced. Your friend may perhaps be surprised that you are taking a forthright assertive approach.

○ Step two: **what**?

(straightforward voice, not aggressive; you are seeking information right now)
"So what happened? Thought we were going to meet here 25 minutes ago?"

Don't show anger or raise your voice at this point. You are just asking what happened. Maybe there is a good reason, maybe not. You're asking.

- Step three: **wondered**

"I wondered where you were and why you didn't answer your cell."

You share what was on your mind. You're not a doormat. You're not an aggressive name caller or bully. You are obviously frustrated. You don't just pass the situation off as if it doesn't matter--because of course it does.

- Step four: **uncover emotion and thought** (some examples)

"I didn't know what to think because I know you like this band."

I was feeling really annoyed because I thought you and I were going to be in the front row when they opened the doors."

"I was thinking of what to do next."

- Step five: **check in** (to move forward together)

"Wanted to check in with you. What should we do now?"

And one more final scenario using the five steps. Your friend borrowed your favorite shirt and got a rip in it and then just gave it back to you without saying anything.

- Step one: **saw**!

"I noticed there was a rip on the shirt I lent you."

Step two: **what**?

"What happened?"

Step three: **wondered**?

"I wondered if you're going to fix it before the weekend?"

Step four: **uncover emotion and thought**

"I was feeling upset because it's my favorite shirt and you didn't say anything about it."

Step five: **check in**

"Wanted to check in with you." (The action now is up to him or her.)

The five step conflict is helpful to practice and have as a conflict resolution tool. You can stop at any step depending on the situation and level of the conflict, or you can go through all steps. Practice saying the phrases in the given scenarios aloud until you feel somewhat comfortable with this five step process. Use it the next time you either feel like lashing out or just swallowing your emotions. With this method of conversation, you stay assertive without losing it or swallowing it. If you need a memory jogger for the steps, use the acronym **SWW-UC**.

Three-step apology

She was late. Again. "Sorry!" He missed a planned event. Again. "Sorry!" She didn't call you back. Again. *"Sorry!"*

Sorry is not the end of the story for you or the other. How trustworthy are you with your friends, family, and colleagues? Answer yes or no if others would say about you that you

- ○ DO what you say you will do
- ○ ARE on time
- ○ HOLD a mental attitude of gratitude and attention

Being habitually late or missing something planned says to the other, "My time is more important than your time."

Habitually making excuses says to the other, "I can't control my life. I'm just a victim to events."

Habitually being distracted gives the message, "I'm not trustworthy in paying attention to this friendship."

An apology is a communication of sincere regret for doing something wrong or something that caused some level of loss, frustration, worry, or anger in someone else. The loss could be of trust, time, or of an object. It's important to know how to apologize more than with just a single word, like "Sorry." Sorry isn't enough most times, and sometimes it sounds flippant like "No big deal" which can make things even worse.

Here is how to give an effective apology in three steps.

Step one: take it beyond sorry

Take the responsibility for being late. Take the responsibility for hurting trust. And then SAY you take it:

"I'm really sorry. I take responsibility for being late and causing us to sit in the back of the concert."

"I'm really sorry. I take responsibility for losing the tickets."

Step two: uncover the loss

When you do something that causes frustration, worry, anger, financial or time loss, you created some problem. If you just say "Sorry," it's not enough because people say "Sorry," for dropping a pen, for stepping on a foot, for bumping in the hall. In some cases, you need more than sorry because you caused some real loss of joy, money, emotion, energy, trust, or time. Here are some examples of using words to uncover the loss.

"I know I made our view of the band farther back than you wanted."

"I know I caused you some frustration because my phone was off."

"I know I ruined your favorite shirt."

"I know you had to wait out here on the street for me a long time."

Step three: fix it somehow

When you do something that causes loss of joy, time, money, emotion, trust, or energy, to someone else, you have a responsibility to fix the loss somehow. Offer to fix it in some appropriate way. Commit to not doing it again.

> *"Let's push forward together to our seats. My treat for a large Frappuccino and dinner after the concert?"*

> *"I promise to be on time next time and have my cell on."*

> *"I will buy you another shirt. I won't borrow your clothes again."*

To remember the three step apology more easily, use a connection to your body.

Put your hand, palm down, out and say: "*beyond.*"

Then flip your palm and say: "uncover."

Finally, make your palm into a fist and say: "Fix it!"

Once you get the 3 parts firm, you won't need the hand movement to remember how to give a solid apology.

You'll have to figure out your own voice and what makes sense in the five step conflict resolution process or the three step apology, depending on the situation. However, these two resources to solve problems can build relationships rather than tear them down. It can help establish assertive expectations without being aggressive or passive, flippant or thoughtless, or hurting others or yourself. This skill makes a difference in managing emotions. Give one of these solutions a try the next time conflict starts to rise up for whatever reason.

Handling Communication Conflicts with Parents

"Life consists of what a man (or woman) is thinking about all day long" (R. W. Emerson)

When people live together in close quarters over long periods of time, problems about space, privacy and lots of other things arise. It just happens with anyone.   Those problems can then take form in emotional words and outbursts.   Anger and frustration can manifest in words of blame or self-justification or denial or even giving up.

What does blame sound like? "You never let me do X!" "You make me mad!" "All he does is annoy me!" "She's always mean!" "He's the reason I can't do Y" "Their behavior is why I act the way I do!" "You always take his side!" "It's all your fault!"

What does self-justification sound like? "You're blowing this incident out of proportion!" "It's just the F-word!" "I get mad because you're not being fair!" "Everyone else does it." "It's no big deal."

What does denial sound like? "I don't know how to change." "I didn't hear you!" "I didn't do what you claimed." "I don't know how X influenced me."

What does giving up sound like? "I'm outta here!" "Yes, I'm apathetic." "I give up; I'm done!" "I'm sick of trying!" "Why knock myself out?" "I can't talk to you!"

These reactions happen with friends and acquaintances. They also happen between parents and their children. It's important to recognize that a parent works to balance anxiety and freedom. That can cause stress. They can also say some things they don't mean. If both of you are in the emotion of rough or hurtful words, it's hard to move into a better communication where some problems can be solved.

What are some counters to these four reactions?

A counter to blame is humility and forgiveness. What does it sound like? "I realize part of this is my fault." "I forgive you and I forgive me for what we said. How about we try again?"

A counter to self-justification is kindness and compassion. What does it sound like?_ "You know I love you." "You do a lot of me and I know you want the best for me." "I know life has been stressful for you lately. I don't want to make it worse."

A counter to denial is truth-telling and integrity. What does it sound like? "I was denying that, but I did know what I was doing." "I made the wrong choice." "I want to get better so you can trust me."

A counter to giving up is perseverance and persistence. What does it sound like? "I'll pick up my clothes and put my dishes in the dishwasher before I leave for school." "I will get my homework done before sports practice so you don't have to remind me." "I will take daily responsibility for X so we don't have arguments so often."

When you seek happiness and satisfaction, don't forget what Eleanor Roosevelt said, "Happiness isn't a goal. It's a byproduct." What did she mean by that? Happiness for self can't be first in your goals because if it is, it won't last. Selfish happiness is based on ego needs. Lasting happiness is a byproduct of better life choices. Improved communication impacts happiness and daily life.

To move communication with your parents into less of an energy-draining event, try some of the following strategies from this book.

1. Start each day with PMA (qualities of a positive mental attitude). Where your thoughts are, your words go.

2. Commit to listening more than speaking or defending. Make listening real listening, not distracted or defensive listening. Just listen.

3. Use the 5 part conflict strategy when things escalate.

4. Use the 3-part apology when an apology is needed.

5. Exchange "but" for "and" in explanations or argument where possible.

6. Use "thank you" more often; express gratitude in words and actions. Gratitude is a power in building happiness and productive relationships.

7. Move from your positioning to see things from their point of view and use calmer words to clarify where there might be a way forward.

8. Focus on what you do have in your life, rather than what you don't have. What you focus on

and talk about often becomes the primary thing in your thought, thus in your conversation and in your life. Will it be lack or abundance? Peace and joy or Chaos? Satisfaction and solutions or despair and stress?

9. Be aware that blaming others, being self-justified, denying your part, or giving up create hurtful words that block constructive conversation. When you hear them in your mind or voice, stop and reflect. Step back and analyze truthfully if you have any part in or have caused any of these reactions too.

10. When you are calm, choose one of the phrases below when emotions heat upI need a few moments to cool off/think things through.

- I can see your point of view; please see mine too.
- What is motivating this concern? Is there a way we can get to a compromise?
- I understand your position on this I think. Tell me more.
- I love you.
- I realize I've contributed to this problem too.
- Let's think of a couple of ways we can move forward from here.
- I'm sorry for all this chaos. Neither of us want it. Let's talk.

Chapter 9
Traps or Assertive Conversations

You know what traps are--they are things you can fall into.
There are four major traps to avoid in the Conversation Game.
Also, in talking, be aware of the effects of passive, aggressive and
assertive conversation.

WHAT ARE TRAPS? Traps in the Conversation Game are just like traps you can run into on a golf course or a hole near the serving line on the tennis court. They are barriers to progress in the game. There are many traps that can be on the playing field, but the good player is aware of them, and usually avoids falling into them.

Trap one: masking

When people are not comfortable with themselves or don't feel they will be liked for who they are, they can consciously or subconsciously put on a mask. People generally put on masks to get along or to be better liked or to cover up who they really are. When a person chooses to put on a mask, sometimes a person hides their true character or deeper values too. When this happens, a player can feel that he or she is compromising the play because he or she is compromising self. It just doesn't feel right.

Some of the masks people wear in the Conversation Game include

o   Acting like a "dumb blonde" or a "wild redhead" or adopting some other "silly" mannerism ("Gee! You mean ME? What do I know?")

o   Acting like a loner or rebel (slouching, hands in pockets, standing on the edge of things, adopting a pouty/frowning expression)

o   Acting like Plum Perfect (very smart, very superior, very together and organized *all* the time, better than you are)

o   Acting like Paul Pleaser (trying to please everyone all the time, changing your opinions depending on who you're talking with)

o   Being a flirt or tease with the opposite sex all the time (standing too close, using body movements to gain attention, touching others all the time, playing one person off against another)

o   Being a cynic (being cynical and sarcastic about everything!)

You have probably seen some of these masks. Perhaps you've tried one or two out on your own face. Have you ever put on one of these masks in a situation, thinking that maybe it would make other people like you more? I know I have. But you know, deep inside, that the mask you are wearing is not who you are. It doesn't feel good and you know that sometime, someone will figure out that you are simply wearing a mask.

In high school, I was talking with some friends once about an event. The talk shifted from the event, to put down and make fun of one person who wasn't there. I didn't feel right about going along with the put-down, but I went along because everyone else in the group did. I had put on a Pleaser mask. Afterward, I thought, "Suppose the person we are talking about heard what we said? Would I be OK with that? Would what I said be something I could stand behind or repeat if the person were standing in front of me?" The answer was NO. In choosing to just go along with what was happening in the conversation, I disrespected my own self. I felt very bad about my decision to support something in words behind someone's back, that I wasn't proud of.

Recently a group of guys got together and put up a website that was extremely disrespectful to some girls they knew. The website got shared beyond their group to lots of people. One of the guys afterward felt so bad. He said, "I thought we were just having fun. I can't take back what we did. I would never have done that to those girls if I had known they would see what we wrote and designed."

Being your authentic self is very important. Your authentic self has values and principles. Your authentic self is unique and intriguing. Your authentic self has power. If you are communicating with someone else and one of you has a mask on, it says to one or both of you "mutual respect is lacking." Why? Because you're either not respecting yourself, you're not respecting the other person, or you are not respecting the relationship that is developing. The more you let the mask stay on, the more uncomfortable it gets.

What's wrong with being who you are? You are unique and your ideas are important. There's no one else like you. Take the mask off and be the wonderful and strong person you are! True friends will respect that choice.

Trap two: not being truthful

Another trap is similar to masking; it's choosing to tell something that isn't totally true—which is of course. . . telling a lie.

When we choose to tell a lie, for whatever reason, it's demeaning to ourselves. Unless we're very good at keeping all the untruths organized, we'll probably get caught up in the web we are making. It's much better in the Conversation Game to be truthful about stories and to be truthful about your values.

To commit to being truthful with self and truthful with others is a position of moral courage. Sometimes it will be hard. If you are having trouble telling the truth, you can choose to be silent. A friend made up this big story about a boyfriend she had met on vacation, what they had done, and how they kept up this long-distance relationship. Over time, it became apparent that there were gaps and contradictions in the stories told, and eventually the story became identified as *a fiction*. People felt betrayed and confused about their relationships with the person who had told the untruths to them. It was just weird for everyone.

Advantages of speaking the truth mean

1. you maintain self respect,
2. you give respect to the other person through your integrity,
3. you won't have to worry about keeping track of what you said to whom,
4. you don't compromise your personal beliefs, and
5. you just feel better.

Will everyone like you all the time? Of course not. It's just a fact to accept and move on with. Will everyone agree with you all the time? No. Will you have to stand out sometimes and have moral courage in your conversation? Yes. But that's OK and that's good. Telling the truth about how you feel and think and what you value can make you stronger.

Move on with the truth rather than using masks or lies. You'll feel better and you'll have the power of personal integrity, even if you aren't always liked by everyone. With friends, you build trust. You'll know people will like you for who you are, not for some one you're pretending to be. Walk your talk.

Trap three: one uppers and jumping

If a listener hears a conversational gambit that was put out by a speaker and then jumps right into sharing their information that is either *much better* or *totally different* from what was put out, it says clearly to the speaker, "What you just said isn't really interesting to me." Or "I have a more interesting thing to say."

Jumping or doing "one up" on the other person, was identified in an earlier chapter as a poor play; it can also be a BIG trap when it becomes a habit. This trap in conversation is very like grabbing the ball as someone else is about to shoot from the foul line in basketball. You also don't jump up and down at that line, shouting, "Look at me! Look at me!" to the crowd watching. One-Uppers make those involved in the conversation and those listening around the edges of the conversation feel like you're doing just that.

What are One Uppers exactly? They are aggressive plays. One Uppers come in different forms, but essentially they are put in play when a player chooses to jump in with something he or she thinks what they want to say will be *more* interesting, They are stealing the time and the

focus, without first giving some atten¹
response to the comments of the person sp⸱

Here's an example   where Jacques ⸱
friends run across the parking lot to join ₅ᵤₘₑ ₅
their other friends.

There's nothing wrong with sharing information on a great day, but in this case, Tom *didn't give one moment of attention* to Jacques' and his friends' day.

Jacques: "Hey, we just got back from the pool!"
Tom: "We just got back from the mall. They're having a great car show there today, and we had a lot of fun hanging out. Brock got to sit in a Lamborghini! Wow, it was so cool!"

What he said was just swept aside and Tom's day was plopped in its place. What can happen with this type of trap, is that the speakers get competitive and try to outdo each other, and the players fall into the trap as a regular occurrence over time.

Here's another example of One-Uppers or Jumping in play.

Tricia: "Our church's youth group went to Peru last summer. It was one of the best trips I've ever had."

Bette: "Oh, well, my sister went to Peru and Columbia. She got to climb to the Inca ruins along this really old trail. They met this archaeologist and got to go into this temple. It was awesome."

Now what can Tricia or Jacques do? They had a story to tell too, but each got ignored, interrupted and one-upped. Tricia in the example above, can continue the game by trying to

- ○ one-up Bette now, or
- ○ she can drop her own story, or
- ○ she can try to get the conversation back to her own story, knowing Bette doesn't seem really interested.

All of these choices are difficult and Tricia is probably feeling somewhat irritated at Bette. If Bette had only followed the Conversation Game and let Tricia shine a bit, asked her a question or two, and THEN put in her own information, things would have gone much better.

Trap four: what do you do with a monopolizer?

What is a monopolizer? It's someone who takes up the majority of speaking space that should be shared. It's someone who interrupts and then puts the focus back on him or herself and ideas. It's someone who goes on and on and on and doesn't give others a turn.

"All Miguel does is talk about himself. It's not fun to hang out with him. I can't say how I feel because I shouldn't have to tell him!"

Why not tell him? What's the problem with that? Suppose you bring this tendency to keep the ball all to himself in this Game, to his attention? What is the worst thing that can happen since you're not enjoying hanging out with him anyway? You could first just say, *"Miguel,"* to get his attention. (Don't try to jump over someone who won't stop talking.)

When you get his attention and he stops talking, you can say what you need. *"When we talk, I need to have some time to talk, too."* Will he get mad? Maybe, but why should you get mad at someone who is giving you constructive criticism? You can bet you're not the only one irritated at his tendency to monopolize.

Here is a two step process to dealing with a monopolizer:

STATE THEIR NAME TO GET THEIR ATTENTION and WAIT:

"Miguel."

SAY SIMPLY WHAT YOU NEED OR WANT TO SAY, FOR EXAMPLES:

"Thanks for telling me about your new car. It sounds great. Let me tell you about the science assignment you asked me about."

- o "Three minutes, and then I need to go to class."
- o "I want to tell you about the dance before I have to leave."
- o "I forgot what I was going to say because you interrupted me." Please don't interrupt me."
- o "Did you want to hear what I have to say about that?"
- o "I want both of us to talk together. It seems I do most of the listening."
- o "Please don't interrupt. I have something to share."

Read these statements above out loud without confrontation/aggression or wounded passivity. Just read them assertively. Are you comfortable with this type of talking? If not, practice will help you to manage a conversation that is being monopolized.

Monopolization can look different in different situations. Someone may add little "huh, so, well, you know, I mean," types of words and phrases to "keep the floor" even if they aren't really adding anything to the conversation. Someone else may *interrupt* and just keep talking on and on without listening to the other person. They may be talking about an idea, about some news, or about themselves, but they don't give others time to be part of the conversation. So, try the two step procedure:

Say their name. Wait to get their attention.
Say what you need or want.

I remember a friend telling me, "*How can you DO that? It seems so hard to tell someone what you need. I don't want people to get mad at me.*" The first time you do something is hard, but it also shows others that you are assertive and are able to play the Game. If you don't ask for your part in the game, you'll always be at the sidelines passively waiting for a turn. It is your choice.

Trap five: playing backward from put-downs

"You always act like such a nerd."

"No one really likes you."

"Your ears are like Dumbo ears!"

"What kind of person enjoys going to a chess club?"

"You are ugly."

"I can't believe you did something so stupid!"

These comments above are all put downs and traps when they become habits in conversation. These are hurtful examples, but of course we all know there are worse examples of put-downs, too. Put-downs can also include nonverbal signals such as eye rolling or mean laughter, or online insults or videos. Put downs are traps, but they will happen. They hurt. Put-downs, even if they are done in a spirit of "banter" are always win-lose situations. One person must be lower than the other, so it's win-lose. When put-downs occur, the recipient often chooses one of these ways to respond:

- o be passive and say nothing, or giggle or laugh. (Being passive is a backward play because the game doesn't move forward equally. Also if you're passive in response to a putdown, it means you agree to take it).
- o ignore what was said. (Ignoring a putdown is a backward play because you're not standing up or responding to something obviously hurtful and it is another type of passivity. Most people may pretend they are not paying attention to a putdown, but they really are).
- o become aggressive and respond with an even larger insult (a backward play because

you're in a trap, both in the same "hole" so to speak, and putdowns escalate).

None of these work well. Your better choice in response to put downs is to *be assertive.*

Being assertive is a good thing. It means standing up for yourself or others without being mean or rude. Being assertive is different from being aggressive. A verbal aggressor actually pushes someone back or aside, or gives the impression of dominating them with words. On the other hand, when you respond with a calm attitude of self-respect and share your expectations for how you or others will be treated, you are **asserting** something about yourself and the relationship you expect.

Assertive conversation

versation involves looking someone ... saying what you believe or need. It ... pect or push someone out of the ... esses the phrases, *"You and I are both* ... *pect. What you have to say is as* ... *what I have to say. When we build our* relationship, *we build it on the rights of both of us."*

Assertive conversation works because those who use it know that managed conflict can be a way to grow. Though good players in the Conversation Game don't seek conflict, they don't avoid conflict when it occurs.

Assertive conversation says to others that we are responsible for our choices and actions and we are not afraid to be who we are. Assertive conversation believes real friendship is strong enough to withstand some disagreement. Assertion means calmly standing up for yourself. Instead of getting into a backward play or getting stuck in a hole, you could practice responding *assertively.*

If an acquaintance uses a demeaning voice to say, *"What kind of person would enjoy going to chess club?!"* You could reply, *"Me. It's fun."* instead of silently feeling bad because someone doesn't appreciate chess.

If someone says with eye rolling: *"You always act like such a nerd."* You could say something like: *"When did you start thinking that I was a nerd? I enjoy graphic design."* You're choosing calmly to address what was said and correct the perceived insult. Sometimes such calm assertion surprises the person who has habits of poor conversation.

If someone says,: *"Where did you get those shoes, the dump?"* You could say something like: "Yeah, that's where I get all my shoes because they're broken in." (You use humor to defuse the power of the insult. This isn't passive--it's responding directly to negative banter. It says to others that what they said didn't bother you and you can turn a joke back on yourself. Humor works if the put down is not very serious. If the put down is about your values or who you are, respond with straight assertiveness rather than humor. Attacks on persons and values aren't jokes.)

If someone says, *"She (your friend) is so ugly."* You could say calmly (not aggressively): *"Here's the deal with me. I don't insult your friends, so don't insult mine."* People will witness that you stand on integrity with and for your friends.

If someone says: *"I can't believe you did something so stupid!"* You could reply: *"Yeah, I did do something dumb yesterday, but everyone makes mistakes."* It's just a fact. No need to get in a defensive posture about it.

The responses above are examples of assertive forward plays because instead of ignoring the put-downs, the speakers respond forthrightly and then are able to move on with the conversation. These plays express values to others .

Self-talk

It's estimated that young people receive *thousands of negative self-comments each week*! WOW. That's really terrible and it's terribly powerful. These negative comments come through texts, online videos, comments from others, looks from others, put downs, ads from media, and from negative self-talk. Negative self-talk affects conscious self-worth.

Dan: "Man, all you girls play really bad."
Paula: "You're such a stupid jerk!! Who listens to you anyway? You boys don't play so good either!"
Salli: (to Dan) "You know that isn't true so why are you saying it?"

Think about the destructive influence of so much negativity. Positive self-talk is very important in the Conversation Game. Positive self-talk deflates the put-downs, whether they come from others or ourselves. Everyone should practice regular positive self-talk—**not** from an egotistic position like,

- o "I'm the greatest one in this room!" or "I'm the best cheerleader around!" but from a position of humility and awareness of personal growth,
- o "I am grateful for this talent and can use it positively."
- o "I'm proud of how I handled that put-down."
- o "I know that many others will be better than I am at this, but right now, I'm trying my best and I feel good about my effort."
- o "I like and value the differences and uniqueness in others and in myself. I'm getting better at talking with other people."
- o "I stood up for myself assertively."

In a good relationship, helpful criticism is welcomed because it encourages us forward. However, too often, put downs are just plain negative. Listen to a negative gambit thrown into play by Rhea and the two different responses (one aggressive, one assertive):

Rhea: "I think all guys want is somebody to wait on them. Guys are all selfish and stupid."
Landon: "You are the one with the problem! Who would want to even listen to your blondie ideas?"
Mandy: "Let's be fair and not put down all guys like that."

Passive conversation

Passive conversation (like giggling, saying nothing, or always agreeing) lets others violate your rights. Passive conversation isn't telling the truth to others. Passive conversation increases stress in a relationship. Passive conversation tries to avoid conflict more than to stand for right or truth. Passive conversational habits can even let you stand by and let someone hurt another person.

You are not a passive doormat. Be proud of yourself and appreciate and support others. Talk positively to yourself--often. Practice speaking out on what is important to you in an assertive way. Know that your ideas are worthy of respect. Don't be fearful of saying what you know is right to say.

Practice getting better at assertive communicatio. , even if you have to start by talking back to your mirror.

Aggressive conversation

Aggressive conversation often develops out of low self esteem just as passive conversation often does. In the previous conversations both Landon and Rhea practiced aggressive communication. Aggressive conversation comes out of the need to dominate or control situations and other people, or be right. Aggression in conversations is more often than not, simply rude.

Aggression abuses others' rights and won't build bridges between people. Aggression uses domination or fear or other cowardly tactics to gain attention or power. From time to time you can see an aggressive person and a passive person hanging out together—one dominates and the other is the one dominated. It's like saying, "I'm big and you are small." It's not an equal relationship. Be proud of yourself and others but don't think you have to be aggressive to be proud.

When we think of aggressive speakers, we usually think of those who have a temper or are loud and interrupt others. In addition, the monopolizers, those who talk too much, can be aggressive because monopolizing dominates the Game and takes over all the talking space. It's an ego problem.

ᴊ progress in the skills of the Game, know ᴊ are worthy of respect and not just --just as others are. Remember that in a good Game has equal opportunity for play and has equal rights. To overcome any aggressive habits, start to practice tolerance, humility, quiet strength, and appreciation for others. Let all the players be equally big.

The play of credibility

Aristotle said, *"Persuasion is achieved by the speaker's personal character. . .we believe a good person more fully and more readily than others."*

When you meet someone and you start to talk together, a gambit is put on the table. There are initial moves and judgments about the trustworthiness of what is said, whether a person is masking or not. Then there are earned judgments that come into play later during the Game about credibility, which is essentially "believability." People gain credibility in the Conversation Game through one of three ways.

Personal competency. That is, they know what they're talking about. They have proved their skill and understanding. They've been there, and because of this, you believe them.

Character. Others gain credibility through character, through who they are, through their trustfulness and trustworthiness. They've been tested and they have passed the test of good character. They aren't masking, they are assertive about their values. They walk their talk.

Strong personality. Still others gain credibility *for awhile* through a strong personality. Using the force of personality is the *least* strong way to have people believe you, because over time personality is just that—based on one fallible person. Any individual can fail to live up to other's expectations. Personal confidence and energy can sag. It's much better to gain credibility that lasts, through good character or real competence. Even better, combine competency and character! With good character and competence, you can join the Conversation Game with calm authority and don't need to dominate the play.

When you enter the Conversation Game from a position of credibility, you can enjoy bringing other people's ideas and comments out onto the table. *You build trust with other people if you are competent and you have good character.* Good character and competence attract respect because people know where you're coming from, and know you don't put on masks. You can increase effectiveness in your conversation by listening, using plays and moves well, by being open, fair, respectful, interested, trustworthy, and empathetic.

WHO CAN YOU TRUST? WHO TRUSTS YOU?

"Just trust your intuition."

"Go with the flow and trust the process."

"I'm sure you can trust him."

Trust impacts decisions as well as relationships. Stephen M. R. Covey distinguishes four kinds of trust: smart trust, gullibility, indecision, and suspicion. Think about your habitual action: do you typically extend blind trust to everyone? Or, do you start most relationships from a position of distrust? How do you get to real and lasting trust in a relationship and a conversation?

The first way is to be trustworthy yourself. How do you do start to become that in other people's eyes?

- Be honest in action, and a person of integrity in your communications, decisions, and choices.
- Do what you say you will do.
- Take responsibility for outcomes and don't make excuses.
- Tell truths and talk straight about hard issues.
- When you can, right what is wrong.

Choose a random person right now in thought. Examine your level of trust. Would you trust that person babysitting your little sister? With your house key? With a secret? With your life? Or, maybe just to be on time for an appointment? Is your gut-level trust high, medium, or low? What data do you have for your gut-level trust with this person? Is it based on level of friendliness or actual experience? Many of us get hung up on how much we like a person. That colors our trust level. It's important to remember that *likeability does not equal trust.*

Here is a short exercise that's only between you and yourself. Just answer yes or no and then think about your answers and why you answered that way. Do you have examples? Is there any area where you need to improve?

1. Sometimes I put on a show or a mask to impress other people.
2. In a group, I'm rarely paid attention to.
3. In different situations and with different people I act and talk differently.
4. Sometimes I put down others in my mind.
5. I have a hard time listening to something I'm not interested in.
6. I am always the person I appear to be.

"Unless you try to do something beyond what you've already mastered, you will never grow." (Ralph Waldo Emerson)

Chapter 10
Keeping Things Going

In this chapter, there are six simple exercises to stop and try out. Practice is important in preparing for the Conversation Game.

HERE ARE TWO excerpts from a Conversation Game. It should be obvious to you by now which participants play the Game well, and which do not. Can you identify some of the good plays and the poor plays?

The first conversation

Andy: "I went to my grandmother's for Thanksgiving."

Sam: "Oh. I went to my aunt's. She lives on a farm."

Where would you go from here, if you were Andy? Sam took the ball from you before even asking you anything about what you said.

The second conversation

Here is another example of a conversation that starts out imbalanced. Krystalle keeps things going with listening and good plays.

Krystalle: "What have you been reading?"

Chandler: (Doesn't reply. Shrugs. Holds up the book title.)

Krystalle: "I haven't heard of that book. What kind of book is it?" (Krystalle isn't put off. She just decides to ask a basic question and check out if he's really not interested in talking.)

Chandler: "Sci-Fi. Has some good characters and twists." (Her interest has brought out two responses from Chandler.)

Krystalle: "Set on this planet?" She smiles. "Tell me more." (She uses a smile and TMM to keep the momentum going. It works, as Chandler adds more detail below.)

Chandler: "I haven't read too much yet, but it's about the future after this earth is destroyed and the people remaining have to make a new life with just a few resources."

Krystalle: "I mostly like biographies, but I'll check this one out in audio for my tablet and listen to it when I run in the morning. We could talk sometime about which character we like best?" (notice, she uses Gimme Two: tells what types of books she likes, she runs in the morning, and clarifies that she's willing to keep the conversation going. Chandler has several clues to move forward and keep a conversation going, if he so chooses.)

Here are a few more short conversations for practice and discussion.

The Third Conversation

What do you think about Andy and Dor's conversational contributions? Do you think Dor's offer is helpful to Sam at this point? What else could Dor do instead of offering himself as an expert? How might you express empathy in a short conversation like this without taking over the conversation?

Andy: "You look kind of thoughtful."
Sam: "Yeah, I'm not sure what to do."
Andy: "Want to talk about it?"
Sam: "Not really. It's just about personal family stuff. Frustrating."
Andy: "I'll just listen if that would help."
Dor: "I have a lot of family issues. Totally been there. I've been through so much with my family. You've come to the right person for advice!"

Let's practice more

Below is another gambit, put on the
friend of a friend of yours.

"Skateboarding is great! It's one of
hobbies now. My friend has a half-pipe
my first board."

Identify two clues that are available for you to
"pick up on" from the gambit so you can make a
play. Then create three questions you could ask this
speaker.

What could be two follow-up questions you could
anticipate from information you will receive?

Let's practice again

"I really like learning about the Greek myths."

Because there's only I sentence, this is harder,
but challenge yourself to create three questions you
could use from this single gambit to make a play.

What might be a follow-up comment or question
you could anticipate creating?

And again

"We went to my uncle's for Thanksgiving. My
cousins were there."

This speaker has given out a bit of personal
information, but it's very vague. Vague gambits like
this one are often more like "touchstones." A
touchstone in the Conversation Game, is a check to
see if the other player is interested enough to ask for
more information. If not, the game is basically

121

r. If the other player does not ask for more detail, that player has chosen the play "*NOT TO PICK UP.*" However, if you do pick up and try to play even with a vague gambit, it's an opportunity to practice honing your own skills in the Game.

Give yourself the challenge of thinking how much you could draw out of a speaker who doesn't give you much to play with. Come up with two questions you might create to make a play from.

More practice

"I saw that movie last weekend with my friend."

Identify two clues in the sentence above, that are available for you to "pick up on" to learn more. Create **three questions** to ask this speaker.

What could be **two follow-up questions** you could anticipate from information you will receive?

Add some more information on your turn, with a **Gimme Two** play. How could you potentially keep this conversation going?

For fun, write out a short dialogue about a specific movie and keep the conversation between two people going for eight lines.

And more

"Yesterday, we talked about Leonardo da Vinci, but I didn't tell you about his backward writing."

Create **two questions** you could ask this speaker.

What could be **a follow-up question** you could anticipate from information you will receive?

Add some more information on your turn, with a **Gimme Two** play. How could you potentially keep this conversation going? You could also use the "Have you ever" play as in "Have you ever tried writing your name backward yourself?"

Another practice opportunity

Here is a more difficult gambit. It includes a personal opinion on a complex and difficult subject. You may or may not know anything about Machiavelli, but see what you can do with this gambit.

"I think Machiavelli's ideas about power are really interesting. Maybe we should try to manipulate other people using fear, to get them to do what we want them to do. It might be easier to get things done."

You will naturally have moves going on in your head after hearing this. You may be shocked. What information do you need to seek to discover the sincerity of this position?

- o Do you think this person is being truthful or sarcastic? Could you ask?
- o What clues would you identify to remind yourself to follow-up on?
- o Can you use assertive instead of passive or aggressive speech?

○ What further information do you need about this topic? What might you say in response? Is there any example of misuse of power you might reference to move the conversation forward from opinions like this?

Take every opportunity to practice improving your Game. When you overhear conversations, analyze them for good and poor plays. When you are given clues, take them as great opportunities for practice. Be aware of, and proud of, your growth in verbal skills. Stop sometimes in your day and notice how you are improving in the various areas of your practice.

Chapter 11
Small Talk Non-Talk

Small talk can be hard because talking about general things can seem boring.
Where do you go next, after the first sentence, in speaking with someone you don't know?

SOMETIMES PEOPLE FEEL awkward meeting new people, or being with groups of people they don't know very well. Part of that awkward feeling may come from a discomfort with part of the Conversation Game called "small talk." Small talk is kind of like an extended greeting. Sometimes it just has back and forth "chat" ("How are ya?" "Ok.") or comments about the weather ("It's so hot today!"). Small talk isn't informational. It doesn't seek detail in response.

The purpose of small talk is to keep things going verbally, by filling up some of the silence. People do this with general comments until a sense of trust is built, or until something interesting comes to the

ne talk that can move things forward.
ll talk isn't great conversation, it's a skill
tant to practice because it is used all the
can use it to your advantage, it can lead
versations and friendships.

It is said that a person must practice a new skill from 25 to 45 times for it to become natural. When you see a basketball player shooting baskets from different distances, over and over and over, she or he is doing that to get the new skill into a natural repertoire. It's the same with the Conversation Game. Small talk is just another "distance" to work at getting into your repertoire.

In small talk, body language, smiling, eye contact and posture are important. You show through your eyes and posture, in a way that is natural to you, that you are listening and that you are interested in being part of the moment and part of the conversation. Small talk becomes the gambit. You have to play off of whatever you're given.

A person who doesn't say much in small talk, or appears not to be interested, makes the other people have to strain to keep the game going. A person who slouches and looks out the window or at the floor during small talk is giving a message, "You aren't really interesting to me. I'm not engaging." A person who doesn't smile or nod from time to time might be perceived as sullen in the small talk process. (Remember the first conversation with Ben in Chapter 1?) Engage fully with conversation, even if it's just with small talk.   You may think small talk is a waste of time and sometimes it appears to be. Still, small talk helps everyone "check out the field" with new players before actually getting into full play. Small talk can be the first interaction you have with someone and first impressions are lasting.

If you are uncomfortable looking Into someone's eyes as you talk, practice doing it. It is said that the eyes are the "windows to the soul." Though it may sound strange, in the Western culture, allowing your eyes to meet someone else's eyes, is saying to them that you are willing to connect with their ideas, and to understand and hear them.

Attach a smile to your practice of small talk. If you're not used to smiling, practice adding a sincere smile from time to time in your conversations. Instead of thinking of smiling as something you have to put on your face, think of it as a natural acknowledgment at the presence of another human being. See what happens.

Sometimes small talk includes introductions. Introductions can work to move smoothly into conversation, or they can get stuck and make people have their own distracting conversations in their heads. In the next example, Paula introduces Mary and Jeff. The parentheses enclose the conversation each person is having silently:

○ **Paula**: "Mary, This is my friend, Jeff." (I think Mary will like him.)

- **Mary: "Oh, Hi."** (He is really cute. I wonder where he's from?)
- **Jeff: "Hi."** (She seems nice, but I always feel so weird meeting new people. I never know what to say.)
- **Paula: "Um, Jeff is from Salida."** (What is the deal here? Here's this really nice guy I'm introducing her to, and all she has to say is "Hi? Do I have to keep adding information?)
- **Mary: "Oh. Hmm."** (Paula probably thinks she has to keep feeding me information. What does she want me to do? Respond to every little piece of information about him? Who cares if he's from Salida? What am I supposed to say to that? He looks nice but I just don't know what to say.)
- **Jeff:** Looks away. (Shifting his position he thinks, 'I'm hungry. I wonder what's on the table? I could get a snack. I don't know what to say to these girls.')
- **Paula: "Jeff's here visiting my cousin."** (Come on, come on, Mary, this isn't supposed to be my conversation, it can be yours!)
- **Mary:" Oh."** (He seems nice, but he doesn't say anything. It makes me feel awkward. He's not even looking at me. I'm kind of irritated with Paula because she keeps telling me all this stuff. Who cares who his cousin is? I won't know his cousin anyway, so now what am I going to say?)

In most conversation, some sort of hidden conversation is also rolling to some extent in thought. If the conversation is a self put-down, the feeling about talking can turn negative. Negative energy and awkwardness could have been prevented in the example above by simply working a bit to

- o uncover clues to work from,
- o ask questions and use plays,
- o using TMM or Gimme 2,
- o smiling sincerely and nodding a bit,
- o and making some of the thinking more visible. For instance, Mary's first thought was "I wonder where he's from?" but she didn't ask.

Remember **SELN**. Use nods during the small talk from time to time. Nods confirm that you're listening and give positive messages about your attention, to the speaker. Try a nod and see what happens with the other speaker's attention.

People often don't like small talk because they can feel dead-ended in it if it goes on too long. Whether or not you are comfortable right now with small talk, some small talk is typically expected after an introduction. Here is an example of when small talk is part of an introduction, but this one differs from Jeff's and Mary's above.

Paula: "Aaron, this is my friend, Jem."
Aaron: "Oh. Hi. How are ya?."
Jem: "Good. How are you?"
Aaron: "Good."
Jem: "This place is crowded. I forgot how much it fun it is to be up here."
Aaron: "Where are you from?"
Jem: "Salida."
     (Aaron could stop here by adding just a one-word
     response like "oh" but he continues the game)
Aaron: "Where's that?"
Jem: "Southern Colorado, kinda near Aspen, but over Independence Pass and more south."
Aaron: "Have you lived there long?"
Jem: "Just moved there last year. It's really kinda hard to live in a small town when you've lived most of your life in a city."
Aaron: "Yeah? I've been here all my life. Tell me a little about what it's like."

Aaron and Jem are on their way. They moved very quickly from general small talk into playing an actual Game using plays. These plays moved the small talk into more "real" talk quickly. Jem can go on to tell a few things about her life in a small town, such as the beautiful hikes, or not having a Japanese course in school, or about how hard it can sometimes be to make new friends. She can ask Aaron about where he's from, his background, his interests. Aaron would then be able to use the clues from Jem to put more plays into practice. Why does she want to learn Japanese? Dos she ski? There won't be any lack of opportunity for further, more interesting conversation if they choose it. This is how friendships start, and small talk is an important part of building words into friendships.

Here is yet another example of small talk when meeting someone. What do you notice about the small talk? Does it move things forward?

Suehanna: "Hi."
Tarin: "Hi."
Suehanna: "I'm Suehanna."
Tarin: "I'm Tarin."
Suehanna: "Where are you from?"
Tarin: "L.A."
Suehanna: "Lived there long?"
Tarin: "Uh uh."
Suehanna: "Are you going to be here for awhile?"

Tarin: "Dunno."

Tarin was hard to talk with because she gave no clues and she didn't ask any questions of Suehanna. Tarin thought of herself as shy, but she came off as kind of unfriendly and standoffish. Suehanna and Tarin's small talk feels more like an interrogation.

It's important to be aware of the silent conversations that are going on in your mind and in others' minds, but not be so distracted by them that they interfere with the Game itself. One person told me she didn't really like meeting new people because it was just too hard. She always felt as if she had to work at it, and it wasn't natural. She would mentally find herself believing like Tarin, that she was just sky and not very good at making conversation. Instead of rejecting conversational opportunities, she could try a few plays like using open-ended questions, giving herself some positive self-talk moves before and during the conversation, using good listening skills and nods, and play *Gimme Two* or clues more often. When she committed these things, it did make a huge differen skills and her feelings, and she was amazed.

Open and closed-ended questions

I found sometimes that when I asked a question in a conversation, there didn't seem to be any place for me to go after getting the answer. My dad would encourage me to ask questions of other people I didn't know very well, and I would say with exasperation, *"I DO. I ask them questions, they answer and then we don't have anything else to say!"* It wasn't till much later that I realized if I had made a small shift in *the way* I asked a question, I could have gone farther with the conversation.   If I had used an open-ended question instead of a closed question, things would have worked better.

What is an open-ended question? An open-ended question is one in which you open the door for more than a single-word answer.   In contrast, a closed-ended question is one in which the answer might be a one-word or short reply. Here are some examples of both open and closed-ended questions or prompts. Identify which are open-ended and which are closed-ended:

- ○ How was school?
- ○ Do you swim?
- ○ Is he your favorite player?

- Did you like the book?
- Why do you think that character is the most interesting?
- How do you organize yourself to get that much homework done at night and still get to soccer practice?
- Tell me how you did your hair. I like it.
- Why do you think the goalie has improved so much?

The first four questions are closed-ended. The last four are open-ended. The answers to the first three questions and the last one, could easily be "Ok" "good" "fine" "yeah" "nope" or something like that. The ball is then thrown back into the court of the first speaker so quickly! The first speaker then has to think of something else to say. Sometimes the speaker thinks of *another closed-question* and the conversation starts to sound like an interrogation:

- "So, you like your coach?"
- "Yeah."
- "What's your coach's name?"
- "Akabi."
- "Who's your best player?"
- "Marco."

Like the conversation with Tarin above, if a talking is starting to feel like an interrogation rather than a balanced and natural talk, shift a couple of questions to open-ended ones. Give the other person a chance to reply with more than one word.

What if you're increasing your use of open-ended questions more, but someone else is using them a lot with you? You don't have to reply with just a word or two.   You can decide to treat a closed-end question like open-ended questions.   Here is an example:

Lex: *"How was science?"*

Chad: *"It was OK."* (now Chad could stop there but he chooses to treat the question as if it were an open-ended one.   He uses the Gimme Two play.) *The new science teacher is cool.   She set up an interesting lab and then we went outside and set up another experiment in the field."*   (Lex now has a couple of clues to pick up on to move the conversation forward.)

One word or one sentence responses

Someone shares some inspiration with you, or shares some important learning experience she had. Whether in text or in person, you choose to reply with one word, like "Fun" or "Wow" or "Hmm." That's it—just one word as a reply.

If someone shares some important information, the ball is in your court. The game is progressing and deepening, and you're standing there without a play. Depending on the level of what was shared, one word responses can even be interpreted as a bit of an insult.

Something is missing. What?

What's missing is perceived consideration for the other's time and shared information. A one word response can be a "stop" signal to continuing engagement. When you are willing to listen, focus, and go beyond one word reactions, you also give other communication like "I care." or "I recognize you gave me something important."

Take time to reflect on what was said, and then give back *at least one sentence (not just one word)* that is a sincere response, or connects with the ideas shared. When you give back communication, not just a one-word reaction, it shows the receiver, you heard them and are choosing to engage longer with them. It tells the receiver you want to share back and maybe give something the person can take back and think about. Instead of responses like "Fun!" "Wow." or sending a sad face icon, if you're stuck try

- o The strategy of TMM, like "Tell me more about how you planned the party."
- o A reflective or thoughtful statement like, "That's good advice. I like the metaphor you used," or "You must have been really hurt and sad after that happened."
- o A thank you with extension, "Thanks for sharing that thought with me. Those ideas will be helpful." Or "Thank you for taking time to find that reference for me." (For more detail on the power of thank you's, check out the chapter on compliments.)

OK, we know that in small talk and banter, o word responses can keep things going. Single words improve in person if you add a nod, eye contact, or smile. But in more important conversations, whether online or in person, one word responses to someone's explanations or important shares, feels abrupt. Choosing to give back one sentence or more, tells the person you really heard them, and invites the other to continue in a conversational relationship.

Chapter 12
After the Hi...

You might be introduced to someone famous someday!
In the meantime, you might want to prepare for encountering anyone.
You can use memory hooks and pictures to remind you of personal
information, and you can practice two simple plays called LDCP
and LDL when someone asks you about a sport, a movie, a class, or
a vacation.

EVERYONE HAS EXPERIENCED some awkwardness in conversation. It's natural and it happens. However, if you are having this feeling regularly in groups of acquaintances or friends, you might want to gather and use some "starters." **"Starters"** are effective moves and plans using mental files of interesting information you have stored up on different topics. Starters can begin a whole conversation or they can be a way to add interest and energize a topic in an ongoing conversation. Here are a few ways I collect my starters, but you will develop your own.

I read a lot and challenge myself to learn about things I'm not normally interested in. Sometimes I watch shows from time to time about people or places, politics, animals, music, current news, unusual events, sports or something I didn't know about before.

I write a few abbreviated notes very small somewhere (maybe on the corner of a notebook, or on a note on my mobile device, or even on my pinkie finger) about something I heard on the news, or read, or even a good joke.

I often attach the information to a picture in my mind or even put a little picture on of my fingers! Pictures really help you remember things longer. I add to my lists over time.   Today, I have a little list of interesting things I can choose to bring up with some people I'm meeting.   I have many of these starters in my mental "back pocket" that I can choose to bring out or not.   I like to keep an ongoing list of information on varied topics as well as a lot of interesting trivia, that I can use anytime with diverse people.

When I was in high school, I used this preparation tool a lot when I was dating. It made me feel more comfortable to be able to pull something to talk about out of my mental back pocket if the conversation started to lag. Part of the little note I have right now in preparation for an upcoming meeting looks like this.

- Gdn

-

- MB

- Lumine

-

OK, this is what each stands for and why I wrote these notes. I know a little about the people I'll be meeting so I want to bring some possible starters. The three letters **gdn** (sounds like "garden") remind me to tell Joe about what I heard about *rooftop gardens* in city apartments because I saw a video clip about urban renewal. I know that Joe's sister in New York City has one. Joe told me he might want to be a landscape architect someday. I also think that story will be useful in a conversation with him or anyone who brings up gardens or flowers or vegetables, or who is interested in gardens and sustainability. I can use this starter a lot because it also includes a funny and detailed story. I might never use it, but I have it if I want to use it sometime.

The second item is a picture of a **windmill**. I wanted to put some information about the windmills out in the Arizona desert in my weekly mini-notes because my friend is going to Phoenix and might pass the field of windmills I read about. I learned how they were designed and how huge they are. That also might come in handy sometime in future conversations with anyone who is visiting the desert southwest, or who is interested in natural energy sources. And, actually, I am interested in reading more about this now. So, even though this information is for me, I might share it sometime. I might not, but still, I have the information.

The third item is **MB** which stands for Myers-Briggs. A friend took the Myers-Briggs personality test and I wanted to tell some of my other friends about it sometime. An upcoming conversation is about breaking through perceptions of self and others so this may come in handy. I wonder if Myers-Briggs preferences affect life choices like career choices or car purchases. I'm still wondering about that.

The next item is a picture I saw of this tiny car called Lumine that is more like a bicycle than a car, but it's all enclosed and has a lot of benefits like great gas mileage and ease of parking because it's so small. I wonder if this type of a car would be popular in the US? Designing these types of cars could be a career opportunity in the future. My friend and a science teacher, both like cars and new technology, so I'll be able to talk to them sometime about this design if it seems natural. It will be a good addition to other conversations with people rs ors of technology. I imagine a luminous ɔ I can remember the name Lumina.

.ɔ next item is a joke about snowboarders, and I have a **red dot** because that's what is in the joke. Lots of my friends snowboard, so I know I can use it. I just had to make a note of it because I might forget it if I don't.

And recently I had a conversation about internet security in the day with an IT expert, and then met a well-known musician in the evening. Both experiences gave me stuff to put in my starter notes.

Anyway, you get the idea. I have lots and lots of starters which I can use some for different groups of people and thus I have a general list of interesting stuff that is in my head that I can use over time. Some topics fade out and are replaced with new ones. However, without actively thinking "This could be a starter for a conversation with X," and making some way to remember and retrieve the information, over time these can be easy to forget.

You might be concerned about using starters and think, "Suppose someone sees me looking at a note on my phone or a drawing on my pinkie finger?" Well, suppose they do? Your next move is to make it natural, "Yeah. *I wanted to be sure to tell you about that and I didn't want to forget.*" WOW! The person will probably feel rather honored that you took time to think of them and their interests in advance and make a note so you wouldn't forget.

Remember, starters can be used anywhere in a conversation. They add fresh, unique information and make you more interesting to those who are talking with you. You can use starter phrases to "get in" to a topic somewhere in the general Game. Some introductory phrases you could use for your starters might be:

- You mentioned cars. Did you hear about...
- I was just thinking about what you said about...
- I know you're interested in ..., did you hear about...
- I've been reading some interesting stuff...
- Have you ever seen...
- You're going to Tucson. Have you visited...
- I wonder what it would be like to...
- I remembered something you might like to know about...
- What we were talking about yesterday reminded me of...
- Did you hear of...
- This reminds me of...
- I heard about...

If you want to polish your Game, you can write out a few short dialogues to read aloud--just for yourself and just to get your mouth and brain in synch and to make talking with other people easier because you've practiced. This may sound dumb or embarrassing, but really the more you practice using starters and practice with plays, the easier it gets when you get into the Game. You can either write a full dialogue or a "cloze dialogue." A cloze dialogue is one in which every other line is not written and you have to decide what to say. Either way, both are useful tools for practice. In the last line of this dialogue, you take over. For more practice, see Chapter 17!

- o **You**: "Hi."
- o **She or He**: "Hi."
- o **You**: "Did you have a nice weekend?"
- o **She or He**: "Yeah. You?"
- o **You**: "It was OK. On Saturday, my sister and I went to see the new ZZ movie. "
- o **She or He**: "I heard that was really good. My brother saw it and said there were a lot of laughs and that the costumes were really strange."
- o **You**: "There was this part where the main character was wearing a bizarre dress that expanded and allowed her to float off into the air, escaping from the thieves. It would have been fun to design the costumes for the movie."
- o **She or He**: "I think it would be fun to design clothes. I could design some really weird stuff. I read about this designer in New York who is using aluminum and linen to make jackets. . ." (reference to a starter)
- o **You**: (so you identified a clue and maybe you have a starter about fashion design? A

school friend designs paper outfits; there is exhibit of shirts made of teabags at the university; highlight weird wedding attire you saw on Facebook... could be interesting!

Being introduced to someone famous

Sometimes the problem with moving past the "hi" comes from talking with someone who is not a peer. This could be a friend of your mom or dad or maybe even someone famous.   It could happen!   It has happened to me.   With a more formal introduction, there are a minimum of three parts you have to include in it.

1. Greeting and repeat their name
2. Offer *your* name (and one optional information bit)
3. Appreciation piece

Many of us are in the habit of only saying, "Hi." and letting it go at that when we meet someone. Try this tri-part greeting instead.

- o "Becca, this is Mr. Gates."
- o "Hello, Mr. Gates." (Greeting and repetition of the person's name.)
- o "My name is Becca-Rose." (offer your name. then you can mention something else about yourself "I'm studying animation," or add something about the person you discovered like "I read about your support of the local Children's Fund.")

to meet you." (Don't forget this small nportant appreciation piece)

ics are easy: just greet them using their your name and maybe a bit of other information, and add the appreciation. You can add more information or an open ended question after that. If you give specific information with poise, good eye contact, a clear voice, a smile and some appreciation, they can then choose to go further. You created a smooth entry and welcoming feeling.

LDCP and LDL

What happens if someone asks you a very wide, but vague open question like *"How did you like the movie?"* or *"How was the concert (game, class or vacation)?"* Because a question like this covers so much, the tendency is to reply with a closed response like, *"Good."* Or a shrug. However, to keep a game going, you can use better plays.

With one of those wide questions about a class, sport, concert, your vacation, or some experience like that, you can use **LDL** to get beyond giving a one word reply. This acronym stands for **Liked/Disliked/Learned.** Imagine you are asked, *"How is school?"*

Instead of just saying *"Fine"* Or thinking *"How can I answer that??"* you can use LDL. You say something you liked, note something you didn't like, and identify something you learned.. This gives the other person a lot of clues to work off of.

*"I **like** algebra this year, but our Spanish class has had three different instructors in two months so there hasn't been much consistency (**disliked**). I'm **learning** a lot about equivalent fractions though with this new method and also got to play drums this year."*

"Do you like the tennis lessons?"

Instead of "yeah." or "they're ok" try LDL: *"I **like** our instructor. She's really skilled and has high standards. I **don't like** our courts. They're really old and cracked so you have to be careful not to trip. I'm **learning** to have a better forehand though."*

Similarly, there are four parts to a question asked about your impressions of a book or a movie. "How did you like the movie?" "How did you like the book?" The four part response will help you narrow the focus. Instead of just saying, *"Good." "OK" or "I dunno,"* use the acronym **LDCP**. These letters stand for **Liked/Disliked/Character/Plot**. So, when you get one of those wide questions about how you liked a movie, you can think "LDCP" and then reply.

You say something you **liked** about the movie.

- o "I **liked** the way it felt like you were actually in the rainstorm at the castle." or
- o "I **liked** how the music supported the narrative." or
- o "I **liked** the action. In one part there was a helicopter escape over the Gobi desert."

- Then, you could say something you **disliked,** such as,
- "I **didn't like** the way the main characters kept talking about old age and dying, when the rest of the movie was funny. That dialogue didn't fit."

Then next, you could choose to keep the Game going with a comment about the characters or the plot:

- *"My **favorite character** was Dennis because he was so sarcastic."*
- *"Jane was cast **just like I thought** she would be in the book."*
- *"The **way the tension developed** really made me feel tense, especially when they had to escape from prison!"*

Also, remember to add some other plays like "Gimme Two" and you'll be on your way to handling those types of vague questions about events, movies or books smoothly!

*With **LDL** or **LDCP** you are in control of the Game and are able to turn a vague, closed question into a more satisfying conversational opportunity.* As in any game, some people are more skilled with throwing you a ball or a question, but whatever type of ball is thrown to you, as a skilled player in the Conversation Game, you'll be able to send an interesting toss back instead of dropping the ball.

Chapter 13
Accepting Compliments and Saying

Accepting a compliment can seem really awkward.
Should you put yourself down if someone gives you a compliment?
Will you feel egotistical if you accept it?
This chapter is short but it has 4 powerful steps for accepting
compliments that work smoothly and information about thank you's.

DO YOU EVER find it difficult to accept a compliment? Here's a four-step basic play that will make receiving a compliment easy:

- You smile
- You say thank you and
- "I appreciate that."
- In your mind, you acknowledge that you are worthy of the compliment.

Here is what is **not** in the play:
- You lower your head

- You disavow the compliment in some way ("I'm not really. . ." "You're just kidding." "Oh, *right.*" You roll your eyes.)
- In your mind, you reinforce that you are not worthy of the compliment though it kind of made you feel good. ("They sure don't know me well." "I'm totally stupid.")

False modesty is a name for the second example. It's worthless. Get rid of that habit. Practice the first play. It's the one with power.

This chapter is a short chapter, but it's very important. Practice the basic play of receiving a compliment till it feels natural. Responding this way isn't egotistical, it's a simple and complete response which includes thanking the speaker for saying it. Once you get the hang of it, you'll feel like someone gave you a gift and you're taking it with appreciation and a smile.

Become aware of how you talk to yourself and be aware of habits you have developed that aren't helping you, so that you can break them. Negative self-talk goes on all the time, everyday, and it carries over into our Game with other people. We need to learn to *accept our good qualities* that others recognize.

We also need to freely offer compliments to others in the context of our interactions. Attention and listening provides opportunities for saying something sincere to someone else that you notice.

- "You are good at this."
- "It's obvious you and your family are close."
- "Where did you learn so much about this?"

All of these phrases are compliments. They are like gifts of attention and recognition. A compliment is a gift you can give or receive. False modesty is like letting the gift fall to the floor. Then the other person has to pick up the gift and try again. When you use the "receiving a compliment" play, you are essentially taking the gift and thanking the giver. That's all there is to it.

Let's assume someone says to you,

"You look really nice today."

- What do you do first?
- What two things do you say to the person next?
- Finally, what do you think or say to yourself?

A team member says, "YES! *You made a great catch!"*

- What do you do first?
- What two things do you say to the person next?
- Finally, what do you think or say to yourself?

Your music teacher says,
"I can really tell you've been practicing your trumpet. You're sounding good."

- What do you do first?
- What two things do you say to the person next?

nally, what do you think or say to yourself?
__ there is to it. Got the idea? You're aware of
__ Jo, now just put it into practice!

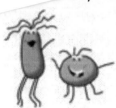

What a Thank You Says

A sincere and specific thank you says:

- I notice your kindness. I remember you.
- I appreciate you.
- I value not only your (gift/lunch) but also your time/ideas/support.
- You are worthy of an ongoing moment of gratitude.
- You have added value to my life.

What the lack of a thank you says:

- I take but don't often give back.
- I simply expect your time, money, support, kindness.
- I'm busier than you are.

Simple phrases like the following mean a lot. Pick one or two and try it out.

Thank you so much for

- your time and help.
- the space you made for me today

152

- how you just made the morning special
- the ideas you shared that help me
- your helping out with (X) today

(It) meant a lot because

- I know you took extra time from your day to meet me
- you took extra time to shop for (or make) something special for me
- What you said helped me to see the situation in a different way.
- I discovered a new place to enjoy in the city.
- I love to spend time with you.

Such communication takes only a couple of minutes but if you're out of the habit of this type of talk, it's worth the practice. Giving kindness and appreciation to someone else can change a little bit of the world.

Chapter 14
What Do Tone, Rhythm, and Pronunciation Have to Do with the Conversation Game?

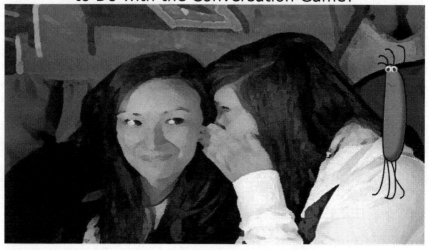

It's about your voice--your own unique voice.
What elements of your voice contribute strongly to conversation?

HAVE YOU EVER spoken with someone whose voice is hard to listen to because their voice is rough, really soft, super loud, flat or unexpressive? Have you tried to listen to someone who mumbles, or someone who breaks words or phrases in a sentence inaccurately? It becomes hard to decipher what is being said because there is essentially another "layer" to get through as you seek meaning in what was spoken.

The tone, the "music" and the variety in what you say, the rhythm and flow of the voice, and the distinct pronunciation of words and phrases all enhance the ideas that are expressed in the

Conversation Game. You are reading this book because you want everything to speak well and you want everything in your conversation to represent you well.

Some people have very pleasant sounding voices and you can listen to them easily for hours. Others have voices that grate, are too high or low in pitch, or are mushy. Some people slur words together, break phrases where they should not be broken or even accent syllables that would not normally be accented: *"Someofus were. . .talkíng with thoseboysover. . .there they said the. . .soccer gamewas . .cancelled."* Whether such speaking is a poor habit or an affectation, it does interfere with smooth listening and comprehension.

One way to check the flow and "music" of your voice is to record your voice as you read out loud. Many people hear their own voices and reply, *"I don't sound like that."* Or *"That isn't me."* We hear our own voices very differently than others do. Our ears are closer to our mouths than other's ears are and we get used to hearing what we *think* we sound like. We often are surprised to hear our voices as they sound to others.

When you listen to your recorded voice, consider several questions:

- Do you stop at the end of a phrase or slur one phrase over into the next one without pausing?

- o Do you speak too slowly, or too quickly, giving most words the same emphasis?
- o Do you include a lot of "space fillers" like *Umm, Uh, Well, 'Kay, Like, You Know,* or other irrelevant phrases or interjections?
- o Is your voice pleasant to listen to?
- o Does your voice express rhythm and variety as you speak or is it basically "flat" no matter what type of speaking you do (responding in a dialogue, telling a story, reciting a poem, describing an emotional event, answering a question, asking a question. . .)?
- o Is your voice too soft or too loud or "just right"?
- o Do you think the recording sounds as if you are muttering or mumbling, or is unclear?

As you listen to your voice, rate it impersonally and without self-justification. If you find some things to work on, don't beat yourself up over the mistakes, take the opportunity to coach yourself and practice a better way. When you have identified any potential areas that need to be worked on, you can use the ideas in this chapter to begin polishing up one of your most important components of speaking: the voice that conveys your clear and skilled conversation.

For practice, record yourself reading the following excerpts. Put the recording aside for a day. Then, make a copy of the readings to give to someone who agrees to be your coach. As you read, coach mark words that are mispronounced hear. Have him or her mark where you also consider the rhythm, pronunciation, speed, and intensity of what you are reading. Have your coach give you feedback about how your voice and tone adds value or takes away from the meaning of each reading. Identify areas that you are strong it and areas that need more practice. Then, using that feedback, do it again and make it better.

First reading, descriptive paragraph

When I pulled my aching body over the final ridge, I saw the shining radiance of the sunrise pouring over me.

"I made it!" I cried to myself. "Over 14,600 feet up in the sky!"

Though my hands were rough and scraped, and though my heart was pounding with exhaustion, I stood up shakily and raised my arms, as if to touch the sun. Would I make it back down the mountain before nightfall since I didn't have enough food or water for one more day? I didn't care because for that one moment, I was victorious!

Second reading, informational paragraph

Scarcity of resources causes governments to make changes. They might shift allocation of goods to a certain geographic region to avoid a famine. They might cut already-low wages so the country can produce even lower cost goods for foreign purchase. Sometimes cutting wages solves the problem of scarcity of resources. People without enough money can't buy needed resources.

Third reading, poem

A thing of beauty is a joy forever:

Its loveliness increases; it will never

Pass into nothingness; but still will keep

A bower quiet for us, and a sleep

Full of dreams, and health, and quiet breathing.
(John Keats)

Each one of these challenging readings should have been read with very distinct intonation, rhythm and inflection, and they should also *sound* very different to you and to a listener. The excitement of the first reading should turn more calm and slower by the third reading. Go back and listen yourself to your first recording of these readings. Be honest with yourself. Read them again and improve the delivery of the three readings in either **pronunciation, rhythm, or tone**. Then, choose some other readings to practice varying your voice with. Try comic books, a classic literary work and a newspaper.

Play with the sound of your voice. Read a poem with a humorous voice, then with a sad voice, then with a flat voice. Read a news item from the paper with pathos, then with a lighthearted voice, then with dramatic enthusiasm. As you play with the many ways you could present different information, think about how much the voice contributes to meaning in reading aloud or speaking—how it adds value and clarity for the listener. Your voice is like a musical instrument. It has amazing potential to express appropriate feelings and provides another layer of interest to the words themselves.

Slash-cueing text

There is a method, called "slash-cueing text" that is simple and works very well when you have to read information aloud. If you find people often ask you to repeat what you said, if you are having difficulty reading phrases together appropriately, or even if you run out of breath and make breaks in a sentence where there shouldn't be breaks (maybe because you're nervous), this method will provide a model and a way to practice gaining more knowledge of how to improve reading text aloud.

What you do is first get something to read. Let's take a short reading from a National Geographic magazine that has some long sentences:

"The overnight ferry to Brittany across the English Channel probably follows a route similar to the one taken by a Celtic saint who sailed to 'Little Britain' from England in the late fifth century to found a monastery."

159

long sentence.   Where do you make can take a breath and yet keep the me people might just plow ahead and as they can until they run out of en stop and take a breath, and continue.   It might sound like this to someone on the receiving end:

"The overnight ferry to Brittany across the. . .

English Channel follows a route similar to the one taken by a Celtic...

saint who sailed from 'Little . . .Britain' from England in the late..."

A better way would be to practice making breaks where they make more sense to your listener. Take the same excerpt.   Put slash marks between phrases. As you read the marked copy, pause very briefly at the slash mark. You'll soon find that you are providing clearer meaning to others.   This method can help when you have to make a speech or read something aloud.   You can also use this method for improving your reading comprehension.

"The overnight ferry to Brittany/ across the English Channel/ probably follows a route similar to the one taken/ by a Celtic saint/ who sailed to 'Little Britain' from England / in the late fifth century / to found a monastery."

Now,/ take something you are reading /and mark it with slashes /so that the reading of the phrases / contributes to and doesn't distract from/ the meaning. Try this/ with a section of a textbook you are reading./ Then,/ read what you marked aloud, / pausing very briefly at the slash marks./   Such practice / increases awareness of the importance of using comprehension breaks/ to enhance understanding for your listeners./ It's especially effective practice too for when you have to make group speeches.

Finally, as you work to make your voice work more effectively for you, don't forget to have fun playing with language and speaking. Just as if you were in a drama class, practice some of the following ways to stretch your voice:

- ○ Show enthusiasm --just with your voice.
- ○ Express joy or sadness --just with your voice.
- ○ Incorporate multi-syllabic words into your conversation from time to time.
- ○ Play with tongue-twisters by saying them loud and three-times-fast.
- ○ At home, practice reading aloud as if you had different identities or are reading with different emotions. Use the slash-cues when reading aloud from a text that has long sentences.
- ○ If you have a chance, participate in a theatrical production or use dramatic voices for fun with a couple of friends.

The more you learn about the voice and its potential expression, the more you can expand your flexible voice and develop your own personal, clear oral style.

Chapter 15
Talking With Others About Ideas that Matter

In class, wouldn't it be nice to be able to participate in group discussions smoothly and interestingly?
What can you look for in readings that promotes higher order thinking and more interesting conversation?

"I hate for the teacher to call on me in English class or in social studies! I have no idea what to say. At least in math you have a clue that there is an answer for the problem."

"Being in discussion groups about novels is hard. I have so many ideas from the whole book that there's too much to say. I don't know where to begin. Usually, I don't say anything."

"I don't know much about what's going on with the news, so I feel kind of 'out there.' How do you get comfortable with talking about complex ideas? I don't want to sound superior with my friends either."

HAVE YOU EVER felt like one of the s
above when you have the opportunity to talk i
or with friends or acquaintances? If we dig in
comments above, the first two speakers seem to be
having trouble with how to put the ideas in their
heads into speech, in a way that makes sense and
contributes to the conversation. They feel awkward.
The third speaker is having difficulty with
background knowledge—not having enough
information about a topic to be an effective
contributor to the conversation.

Let's take the first challenge first using a novel
study. How do you organize all those ideas you have
in your head? A mental organizer of some sort
helps you to have a clue about what might be
expected in the conversation. A mental organizer
can help all those ideas that are floating around in
your head, find a place to land, so you can retrieve
them when you want to. When a novel, play or
movie is being discussed, a mental organizer can be
a picture, a table or chart, a Venn diagram or even
words inside a colorful bunch of balloons. The shape
isn't the most important thing. What a mental
organizer does is provide a place for all those ideas
from the book or movie to become organized and
thus it also provides a place in your memory with
specific resources you can draw on in conversation
and discussion.

In this chapter are two tools you can use to help you prepare to enter into discussion on just about any story in literature, or any movie made from a novel.   Think of the list of following questions as a tool such as a detective might use to seek out information.   You choose one of the categories that sounds interesting, first.   Then, in a discussion, you can

- o Choose one question to think about more in depth, such who intrigues you most in the story, or Choose to think about all the questions in a category, like the setting, or,Think about comparing across categories. For instance, you might think how the main character, the setting and the conflicts relate in some way.
- o You can connect questions or add more information to the margins using bubbles, as you read and discover patterns or "aha" moments.

A mental organizer for a conversation about literature or movies

(If you don't like lists, transfer the categories to cells in a table, or make colored bubbles for the categories and associated questions.) Start with one question and then see if there are other interesting connections you want to explore.

Main Characters

- List the main characters. Is there any character you like best?
- What draws you to her or him?
- Why is he or she interesting, in your opinion?
- What type of person is the character you chose and how do you know?
- How was this information revealed? Was it revealed through dialogue or through actions over time?
- Do your character's beliefs, values or personality change over time?
- How does this character contribute to the story? (Without him or her, would the story be less interesting? Why?)

Setting
- Where does the story take place? Can you state the main setting and the subordinate settings of the story?
- Why do you think the author chose this setting?
- What does the setting look like?
- Is there a lot of detail and sensory information or not?
- What stands out?
- Is the setting important to the development of the story or the development of the characters?
- Does the time of year make a difference?
- Does the setting have any metaphors or symbols that contribute to the story?

Plot
- o What is happening in the story? Can you summarize the general plot in a couple of sentences?
- o What is most interesting to you in the story's development?
- o Is the plot simple and direct, or is it complex with lots of twists and turns? What turns and twists were most interesting?
- o If you were to draw the plot, what would it look like?

Conflicts
- o Where are the conflicts in this story? (They can be between one or more persons, between a person and something outside of himself or herself including nature, or even an inner struggle with himself or herself or with his or her values in situation.) What do you think your character is experiencing?
- o Compare and contrast this book to other ones you have read. Are there similarities or differences with the kind of conflicts that are happening?
- o Do the conflicts make you think more deeply about the story?
- o Do you enjoy the conflicts or are they unsettling?
- o Does the conflict "hit home" or is it something new in your experience?

Extending Text
- o Find a quote from your character that reveals something about your character, about relationships in the book, or about life in general.
- o What is most interesting about that quote? Why did it stand out to you?
- o Does the quote remind you of another book you've read or movie you've seen?
- o Find a descriptive paragraph that you like. Why do you like it?

Style And Development
- o What can you say about the style or structure of the book, or the development of the story?
- o Does the style of writing or any dialogue contribute to or detract from the story's development?
- o What stands out to you about the author's writing style that is similar to, or different from, another book you've read?
- o What in the story's general development is in contrast to another book you've read?
- o Is there any figurative language that stands out?

Also remember LDL (liked/disliked/learned) in your conversation.

With this mental organizer at least partly filled in with some notes, you will have a lot of things to talk about in a group). Following are examples of effective and ineffective plays in literature discussions. The first scene is a study group. Ivory and Jerry are to have a discussion using a worksheet given to them by the teacher.

Ivory: "Jerry, what stood out to you in the first act of Hamlet?"
Jerry: "I dunno."
Ivory: "Well, what character is most intriguing so far?"
Jerry: "I dunno.. This is boring."

Where do you go if your conversation is stuck like this? Another idea to help you glean ideas from readings for more interesting academic discussions, is to *seek principles of design* (identified here as CE-UMP) that are behind artistic works. CE-UMP stands for **C**ontrast or compare, **E**mphasis, **U**nity, **M**ovement, or **P**atterns. Choose one of these to think about as you read.

Contrast or Compare

Look for contrasts or comparisons in the story. You might look for two characters who are very different. Maybe one character shows off the qualities of another character. Maybe you'll discover a contrast in the settings or even between a movie and a book version of the same story.

In the arts, seek contrasts that stand out and seem to have meaning to the interpretation of a single artist's work. Or, compare a musical composition on a theme but by two artists. Contrast elements of various movements over time.

In social studies, consider different time periods and their effects on the development of a political movement.

Emphasis

What does the author of a literary work seem to emphasize? What examples can you find in the work to support your idea?

Where is the emphasis in a musical score and what effect does it have on the whole?

What emphasis is placed on certain parts of a political solution involving two countries at a period in time?

Unity

What ties a book or movie, time period, design or theme, together? What gives it "form" and "structure?" What unifies a composition? What unifies a new country's leadership?

Movement

What seems to move the story, or the event, or the design of the artistic work along?   Is the movement slow or fast in your opinion?

Patterns

Are there any patterns, metaphors, symbols, etc. that you can find in the story that stand out to you with meaning?

Is there any symbolic meaning in the design of an artistic work?

Is there any pattern in selected famous original speeches?

The following conversation doesn't use CE-UMP and feels kind of "flat" without anywhere to go.   It stays at the level of "I like" and "I don't like."

Laura: "I like this book. I like Elizabeth."
Lisa: "Why?"
Laura: "She's just interesting to me."
Landon: "I liked the movie better."
Landon: "I think the book was better."
Laura: "I didn't."

So to improve this type of flat discussion, the students can use questions from the mental organizer or the strategy of CE-UMP.

Still another way to talk about things you are learning (especially information about historical figures, discoveries, artistic expression, or inventions), and to get beyond the basic level of

what you like or don't like can be called
"Habits of Mind."   Think of how a his
musician or a scientist might view parts (
Each would select and view things diffc.
Habits of Mind of a great musician would be differc..
from the Habits of Mind of a great scientist.   Here
are a few ideas to get the conversation about history
or science, art, poetry, or music, going in a more
interesting way:

- o Think about how events in the past were
  experienced by those people in the past,
  instead of how we see things from our
  perspective now.   (For instance, consider a
  Berlioz concert, Rococo design, the
  suffragettes' cause, the discovery of radium,
  the poetic structure, the Impressionist
  movement—we study about these things now,
  but how were they experienced and thought
  about in the context of the past?   What was
  the state of thinking in the society in the past?
  What built the capacity for the changes that
  occurred?)
- o Think about how some ideas in the field
  change while other ideas continue. What ideas
  are enduring and what ideas have been revised
  in an area of study in which you are
  interested? (People don't use bloodletting with
  leeches. Quantum physics is quite distinct
  from Newtonian physics and influences how we

see space and time. What are you discovering?)

- Think of the importance of personal character in past events, biographies or discoveries. How did personal character (positive or negative qualities) impact or interfere with the situation and outcomes of the event? What qualities were similar in two disparate historical figures or artists and what qualities were distinct?
- As you read biographies or learn about discoveries, think about what ideas and discoveries are continuing to be important and lasting in our world today, which people's ideas and discoveries had intense impacts on a time period or place, and which ideas or people were relatively inconsequential, though they seemed important at the time.

Reflect on what you notice in the next two high school dialogues:

First example

Mandisa: "What do you think about this outsourcing of jobs that's going on?"
Howie: "I don't know. What do you mean?"
Mandisa: "I mean jobs are going overseas."
Howie: "I guess it doesn't matter. I don't know. Everyone needs jobs."
Mandisa: "I'm concerned that I won't have a job when I graduate."
Howie: "Oh, you will. Hey, is that Mark over there? Let's go and see how tryouts went."

Second Example

Greg: "What do you think about this outsourcing of jobs that's going on?"
LaDell: "I think it's kind of scary. I mean we get products cheaper to buy, but in the short term we lose jobs so we get a bigger hit. People without jobs can't afford to buy the cheaper things anyway." (pros and cons contrasted)
Greg: "Yeah, that's true. But why did you say that in the short-term we lose jobs?" (He's essentially asking her to tell him more.)
LaDell: "I think in the long term, there will be new jobs and new technologies and things will adjust. It's the transition period that is difficult." (she's sharing her emphasis on future-thinking.)

ɔnder about the importance of having ᴊ knowledge on a lot of topics. ⁄ knowledge is extremely important in the ᴊiscussing important ideas. If you want to better skills and be a player of excellence in tn◡ ⁄nversation Game, learn more about a lot of things. As you are learning, even if you don't know a lot about a certain topic, you can still use the good listening and talking plays in this book to keep the game going with interesting people as you gain more information.   You can also use starters to move a conversation along (as mentioned earlier in this book.)

Know that you *will* be perceived by your speaking and listening ability. The quality of your thoughts is expressed in your spoken words with others. Scholarships, job offers, research opportunities, and raises will be increasingly competitive in the world of tomorrow.   *Many futurists state that good communication skills will be one of the determining factors of personal success.*

Go back and review a chapter or two before you move to the next one. Highlight a conversational strategy and commit to practicing it at least 10 times in the next two weeks.   Choose a personal coach who has good conversation skills (perhaps a teacher, debate team leader, friend or relative who has good conversational skills).

Let your coach know that you are on a personal improvement plan to hone your speaking skills so that you can be a better player in the Conversation Game. Share this book with your coach so he or she knows some of the ideas you're working on.

Ask your coach to evaluate honestly how you are doing in different types of conversations, and ask him or her to give you feedback about how you listen and how you play the Conversation Game.

Continue to learn more about the world and its ideas—even things you don't think you're interested in right now. The more background knowledge you have, the more "Velcro" you have in your mind so that other ideas and patterns can stick and connect. You also have more resources from which to draw connections as you converse with diverse people.

Know that you can take on and meet the challenge of improving your critical communication skills! Commit to the practice it takes. Building your personal competency through knowledge, builds your credibility and your relationships, and ultimately life success.

Chapter 16
Your Turn

We've been talking about the importance of practice, so now it's your turn to identify what works and what doesn't work in some conversations.
How could you make the conversations better?

WITH YOUR NEW conversational ability, identify what is not working in the following actual conversations. It could help to read them aloud.

1. Jeff And Maria

Jeff: What's wrong?

Maria: Oh nothing much. My arm hurts a little. I just took a turn too fast on the bike trail.

Jeff: Oh, you should go to the chiropractor on Drake Road. He's the very best. I mean it, you should go to him. He will help you.

Maria: I'm relaxed (laughs). I just took that last turn too fast, but I'll be ok. Thanks.

Jeff: No, I mean it (pointing at her).   You should check your arm out at the chiropractor. It's what you need. He will fix you up.

- What is one problem you see in this short conversation?

- How might Maria be feeling after this conversation?

- How might Jeff have improved his effect on Maria?

- How could Jeff show he was listening rather than just telling?

2. Louisa And Mike

Louisa: OH. Mike, Hi!   I just have to tell you! I get to go to New York City and spend a week in lots of the art museums! It's going to be **sooooo** great!   I wanted you to know!   I haven't seen you in awhile but I wanted you to know because I know you'd really appreciate doing something like that.   I'm going to the Metropolitan—just so excited! Well, what have you been doing?

Mike: I just got back from Santa Fe...

Louisa: Oh yeah, there's a lot of good art in Santa Fe, too. I'm going to the museum on Native American art out in New York. It's the best Native American art museum.

Mike: Yeah. Have fun.

- What is the main problem that happened in this conversation?

- How do you think Mike feels after this conversation?

- What might he think about Louisa?

- How could Louisa have improved this conversation?

3. Misha And Bercy

Misha: Love your skirt!

Bercy: Oh, I found this in the back of my closet and just haven't worn it in awhile. It's old.

Misha: Still...love it! Great color! Really, it's great.

Bercy: Not really. Just an old skirt.

Misha: Goes well with your tights.

Bercy: Right.

- What do you see as a problem in this short dialogue?

- What are Bercy's comments saying to Misha? What do you think Bercy might be thinking about Misha?

- Could the conversation be improved? How?

- Could Bercy just use the Accepting a Compliment and thank you play?

4. Dave And Claude

Dave: So what do you think?   You like it, right?

Claude: I dunno,

Dave: This is the poster! You gotta buy it.

Claude: I'm looking for Tr...

Dave: No, this is the one. You need this one. Take it; Sheila will love it.

Claude: Not sure, I...

Dave: You need **this** one.   You know I'm right.

Claude: Ok...

- How is Claude probably feeling about his friend Dave?

- What could Dave have done to improve the balance in the conversation?

- What could Claude have done to be assertive instead of passive?

5. Candice And Vanessa

Candice: What do we do now?

Vanessa: We put the mixture under the Bunsen burner and watch for the color change. Oh look, it's happening!

Candice. Yeah. Mmm. I wonder if Nick is going to be at the dance?

Vanessa: Maybe, probably. Are you recording what's happening on the lab report?

Candice: What should I write?

Vanessa: That our first mixture changed to blue in 12 seconds!

Candice: Yeah, I saw. So why do we need to write it? It's boring.

- How do you think Vanessa is feeling about Candice as a partner?

- What could Candice have done to improve the conversation and her focus?

6. Frankie, Abe, And Jeanette

Frankie: Who is that girl?

Abe: That's my cousin's friend. Hey, Jeanette, this is my friend Frankie.

Frankie: Hi.

Jeanette: Hi.

Abe: Frankie just moved here from Durango.

Jeanette: Oh.

Abe: Jeanette goes skating with Mary and me.

A Teen's Guide to the Conversation Game

Frankie: Cool.

Abe: Frankie does hang-gliding.

Jeanette: Oh. Wow.

- What is one problem in this conversation?

- How could Frankie or Jeanette improve the conversation?

- What do you think Abe might be feeling about being part of this conversation?

- Do you have any idea about what Jeanette's thoughts of Frankie might be?

7. Bob, Milly, And Houston

Bob: Oh man, Houston, how did you learn to make your guitar sound so out of tune?? You can't even harmonize with me.

Milly: (giggles) It's ok....

Bob: It's SO NOT ok, what are you saying? What's wrong with your ears? This is MY band and I say you stink, and I say Milly can't hear.

Milly: It's ok, Houston.

Houston: You think your voice is better? Fernando should be the lead. It's your voice that is the problem, not the guitar or the music.

Bob: Milly, what are **you** smirking at?

181

Milly: Nothin, Bob.

- What is contributing to the way this conversation is falling apart?

- Who is the most aggressive in this conversation?

- Who is the most passive?

- How could each of the players improve their conversational interaction to be more effective as a group and as individual speakers?

8. Fabio And Mario

Fabio: I had a ride in my uncle's Camaro! It's black and ...

Mario: Yeah, I had a ride in my brother's friends' **Cayenne,** can you believe it? I really got a ride in one of **those**! Talk about FAST, up to 140 mph and 300 horse power! Beyond fine! And the interior. . .just so fine.

- How do you think Fabio is feeling about Mario after just this bit of conversation?

- How could Mario turn it around a bit?

9. Francie And Les

Francie: Hey!

Les: Where have you guys been?

Francie: We just got back from the pool.

Les: Oh. **We** just got back from Water World. What a great bunch of pools and slides and waves! We had SOOO much fun and then we went and got tickets to the concert tonight.

Francie: No way!

Les: Yeah! So... was the pool fun?

Francie: Yeah, we spent a couple of hours, I got burned ...

Les: Yeah. Well, the concert tonight will be so great. I can't believe we got tickets!

- What happened in this conversation to make it feel unbalanced?

- What could Les do to improve the conversation?

This next one is for you. Just listen and watch conversations going on around you—in the grocery store, in the hall, on a subway, in line for an event, in a restaurant. Choose one. Analyze what is working and what isn't and why. How are the tone, body language and listening skills impacting the conversation you're analyzing? What is working? What could be done better? Be a language detective and apply the good things you notice to your own repertoire.

Chapter 17
Feedback is the Breakfast of Champions

Feedback! Feedback is critical to every great player.
Feedback in games and sports, in music, and in conversation is
critical to growth and improvement.

DURING THAT PANEL presentation on a current issue in Washington DC that I mentioned in the first part of this book, I wasn't worried about the TV cameras or the people standing around that I would talk to afterward. Why? Because I had clearly in my mind a framework of what I wanted to discuss. In the past, I had worked on the tone of my voice, its rhythm, and my word clarity, so I felt OK there. I was aware of the importance of eye contact, nodding, and listening. To prepare for the presentation, I had used mental organizers, and awareness of some Habits of Mind. I was ready to give and receive open ended questions. I was used to seeking clues and making plays like Gimme Two and TMA. I had some starters ready for reference. I had defined some LDL areas on the topic. In short, I felt ready to play.

When you start to practice using the plays in this book, people may think you are just a natural at conversation. Only you, like any good player in a sport, know the extent and work and practice behind the "natural" outcome.

You might think that talking to large groups is the most difficult type of experience. But, for me, one of the hardest things in the Game used to be talking one-on-one and keeping a flow of conversation going using open-ended questions and active listening. I worked on that area. *I'm still working on that area.* Instead of avoiding these challenges in areas where I'm less comfortable, I take them on. These opportunities build my skill and confidence. I take the opportunity to practice wherever I can, with waiters in restaurants, with people of different ages, on buses, at events, and with friends. I'm glad when I notice improvement.

One time, I had to talk to some local dignitaries and be able to participate in small talk with various people at a party afterward. I chose to use SELN, active listening skills, and I made sure I had background knowledge of the people and events impacting the day that I could use as starter topics. I chose not to use a mask to get attention. I determined to be a good listener in discussions. In the conversations, I was able to use nods, Gimme

Two, LDL, and TMM a lot with different people. I listened more than I spoke. I checked my tone and voice quality to be sure I was clearly received. Overall, I was surprised that I felt comfortable with those relatively famous people, because I had some simple and effective strategies to keep things going smoothly.

As I think of all the opportunities I've had to speak and to improve talking in my life and career, I have to smile because things were so very different in how I spoke to people years ago, when I would have literally escaped from the room to avoid having to talk with strangers or give a speech. Playing a good conversation game has helped me get a good job, get solid raises, and have opportunities I wouldn't have had without the skills.

Because practice with the moves and plays in this book has helped me, I know they can help you. You're reading this because you want to polish this crucial area of your life. You're already ready to move off the sidelines into the Game.

So, I offer you a bit more basic practice. As you practice, the gambits and plays in the Conversation Game will become easier. You don't learn to play golf by just watching; you don't learn to swim by just watching; you don't learn to play cello by just watching. Get the idea? As you get more familiar with the Conversation Game, you can write down more complicated and actual dialogues to practice, including difficult ones you've run into, and possible responses. The exercises below are just really basic ones to get you started. Conversation really becomes like a fun game that you can break down and practice and then build upon!

Practice is the breakfast of champions and feedback is the energy you get from that breakfast! I like feedback, too. Let me know if you like this book and how it has helped you. Let's continue talking.

Here are a few practice exercises for you to make contact with the Game. Use these opportunities to "think on the spot" and have a short conversation with a partner. If you go to **www.RubyMountainPress.com** you can hear audio of these six practice sessions.

Small Talk

"Hi, how are you?

You:

"Good."

You:

"Not doing much today."

You:

Argument

"Just because you like the Yankees doesn't mean they're the best team."

You:

"No Way! They have a lot of problems this year!"

You:

"The Red Sox are hitting way better."

You:

"Whatever."

You:

New Acquaintance

"Hi. I'm Drew.

You:

"You like golf?"

You:

"I play with our school team."

You:

"Do you play Frisbee golf?"

You:

Compliments

Compliment: "You did great."

You (to the other person):

You (to yourself):

Event

"There was a mime show downtown yesterday. Mike and I watched it."

You:

"I really like mime."

You:

Book Share

"I just finished that book. Thanks for giving it to me! It was great!"

You:

"I don't usually like sci-fi, but that setting, WOW."

You:

Put Downs

"Class was so boring."

You:

"Rex acts like he's really into algebra."

You:

"How can you be friends with such a nerd?"

You:

Conversation is all about building relationships, connection and friendships. Communication skills are in the top three skills needed for future success in almost any field, and in leadership. In addition, there are academic standards and expectations for good communication. Seek out opportunities to practice different types of conversation with different people. Seek feedback and give yourself honest feedback on how you're doing.

Now that you have finished reading this book, go back to the beginning and read bits again in whatever order you want to, and practice as you go.

Continue to use the book as your personal coach.

Then, get out in the Conversation Game and have a blast!

Dedication

To Steve who takes on the hard work without complaint, and always has my back.

To Becca who inspires me with her creativity and leadership. and is committed to being an effective, caring teacher.

To Mandy and Travis who motivate me to work for the children of the future, and for Chace and Declan to enjoy when they're older.

And, to all of you, for your desire to build your capacity and success in the Game.

About the Author

Kathryn Knox has spent her professional life in education.   She has been a French and English teacher, an ELL teacher and coordinator, a principal, a director, a trainer and a national consultant, and will always be an educator and writer. She has been a speaker and presenter and has written several other books.

Her favorite activities include taking road trips with her husband, helping youth develop their innate abilities, hanging out with her daughters and family, cooking, jumping on a trampoline, enjoying and trying to do some basic ballet, and making beaded tapestries. Visit www.RubyMountainPress.com for more books, blogs, and a contact link. She'd love to hear from you!

NOTE TO PARENTS

"Employers in the 21st century economy need workers with people skills that enable them to communicate effectively."

"While development of social skills may be an important educational goal in itself... (communication) is also logically related to academic performance." (University of Chicago Consortium on School Research, June 2012)

Interpersonal qualities are included in recent research on academic success using non-cognitive elements of cooperation, assertion, responsibility, empathy--all expressed to a great extent through language. This book supports using language to develop these qualities and skills.

NOTE TO TEACHERS

The skills students develop in The Conversation Game support oral communication standards and benchmarks such as these below.

• Oral communication is used both formally and informally.

• Students speak clearly at an understandable pace, and with appropriate volume and pitch.

• Students distinguish levels of formality with different audiences.

• Students use language to converse with diverse people and keep a conversation going.

In addition, <u>A Teen's Guide to the Conversation Game</u> supports Common Core Standards for oral communication:

- To become college and career ready, students must have ample opportunities to take part in a variety of rich, structured conversations—as part of a whole class, in small groups, and with a partner—built around important content in various domains.

- They must be able to contribute appropriately to these conversations, to make comparisons and contrasts, and to analyze and synthesize a multitude of ideas in accordance with the standards of evidence appropriate to a particular discipline.

- (They must be able to) prepare for and participate effectively in a range of conversations and collaborations with diverse partners, (formal and informal interactions), building on others' ideas and expressing their own clearly and persuasively.